Initiation into the royal art: a closed body of knowledge, sacred to the elect.

CABALAH PRIMER

INTRODUCTION TO ENGLISH/HEBREW CABALAH

By
HENRIETTA BERNSTEIN

DeVORSS & COMPANY
P.O. Box 550, Marina Del Rey, CA 90294

Cabalah Primer, Introduction to English/Hebrew Cabalah

Copyright © 1984 by Henrietta Bernstein

Second Printing, 1987

ISBN 0-87516-526-5
Library of Congress Catalog Card Number: 83-72946

Manufactured in the United States of America
DeVorss & Company, Publishers

To
MOSES
I gratefully dedicate this work

TABLE OF CONTENTS

8

INTRODUCTION

INTRODUCTION

e have a very short stay on the physical plane of existence. It's kind of like an airport that is fogged in. You go there and plan to take right off, and find out that the flight has been cancelled for fifty or sixty years. Now, what are you going to do with that time? Are you going to sit around and gripe and groan, or are you going to do something with it? Well, a number of us will go to the bar, and sit there in life's great bar as we chatter idly with all of the people and waste our time in the illusion. Some of us will read a book, others will wander around, and one or two of us will have the intelligence to go home. Now we can always think of life as that airport; everybody is trying to get somewhere—but it's fogged in, and nobody is going anyplace. The purpose of Cabalah is to show us the way home.

Cabalah comes to us to expand our universe so we can expand ourselves. For two thousand years or more we have had this cipher code for the interpretation of Scripture. We find here astounding hidden wisdom. Every age has seen it through its own eyes, but this book is an attempt to cast it into twentieth century terms, introducing new dimensions, so that it may flourish for another season.

Unlike other books on the Cabalah, this effort is a commentary on the *English Cabalah*, and how it enables *Hebrew and English systems* to work together. The basic aspects of the Cabalah are amazingly simple, but in our present civilization we have lost sight of them because we have divorced letters from numbers. The ancient Hebrews had no separate system for identifying numbers from words. They understood the principles of *Phi*, the Golden Mean of the Greeks, but Cabalists today are unaware that this was a part of the secret "Unwritten Cabalah."

Today Cabalists are living in the Hebrew past. But language has changed, and mathematics has added the decimal system to replace the laborious mathematical computations of the ancients. Therefore, we must move into the Now.

In this volume you are being introduced to a new cabalistic system. That new system is the *English Cabalah*, using the *English language* of today to help interpret the wisdom of the past. It was first brought forth by William Eisen in 1980 with Volume I of *The English Cabalah*. This was followed in 1982 with Volume II, and his latest effort, *The Essence of the Cabalah*, is being published in 1984. These books present entirely new concepts, and they most certainly open the door to the hidden wisdom contained within the English language. Therefore in the course of this instruction, certain passages from these volumes will be given verbatim, inasmuch as this book is an attempt to simplify the *English Cabalah* for the average reader. Isn't it wonderful that the mystical knowledge within Scripture can now be deciphered—not by some new complicated code—but by our own language, the English language of today?

The Hebrews translated the 22 letters of their alphabet into numbers. We will do the same with the 26 letters of the English alphabet. The *Hebrew* and *English* aspects of the Cabalah will be explained along with the *Tarot*. These three systems enhance each other, and the combination of all three is the most comprehensive way to study Cabalah.

The mathematical system of *Phi* is new to our present-day scheme of Cabalah. These principles have been lost to the world for a long period of time. Yet, the ancient Hebrews understood *Phi*, as we will demonstrate in this volume. It is the *English Cabalah* that brings this sytem to us again at the beginning of the New Age.

As we approach this new Space Age, we begin to understand that everything in life is mathematical. All action on the physical plane obeys distinct mathematical laws and cycles. It is as Pythagoras once said, "there is absolutely nothing in nature that is not affected by definite numerical influences." Moreover, mathematical expressions used every day in physics, life, and nature can be translated into words of the Engligh language; and once interpreted, they state the simple truths of life. Thus we find that the English language is a divine language, and one that has evolved under Divine Guidance.

The "Unwritten Cabalah" of the Hebrews was never given out to the general public, and it was only understood by the priests or the higher initiates into the Mysteries. Consequently, it was never written down but only hinted at. It seems that because it contained so much wisdom and power, they wouldn't reveal it. But in this present volume you will be introduced to one of the main aspects of the so-called "Unwritten Cabalah," namely: the laws of *Phi*. But again, this book is only an introduction, the real "essence of the Cabalah" lying in the aforementioned three other volumes.

What Cabalah teaches may have been best said by Albert Einstein in the following story: When Einstein was living in Princeton, he had a touching exchange of correspondence with an ordained rabbi. The rabbi had a young daughter whom he sought to comfort over the death of her sister. No source of relief for her sorrow was found in traditional religion, so recourse was made to the scientist.

Einstein wrote in reply: "A human being is part of the whole, called by us Universe, a part limited in time and space. He experiences himself, his thoughts and feelings as something separated from the rest—a kind of optical illusion of his consciousness. This delusion is a kind of prison for us, restricting us to our personal desires and to affection for persons nearest to us. Our task must be to free ourselves from this prison by widening our circle of compassion to embrace all living creatures, and the whole of Nature in its beauty. Nobody is able to achieve this completely. But the striving for such achievement is in itself a part of the liberation and a foundation for inner security."[2]

Now let us grow in light. It is my joy, my pleasure to bring you these new thoughts for the New Age.

Henrietta Bernstein

NOTES

1. The frontispiece is from "Theatr. Chem. Britannicum," reprinted in *Alchemy*, by Johannes Fabricius (Copenhagen, Rosenkilde and Bagger, 1976) page 12.

2. The quotation of Albert Einstein is taken from *Clausen's Commentaries on Morals and Dogma*, by Henry C. Clausen (The Supreme Council 33°, Ancient and Accepted Scottish Rite of Freemasonry, Southern Jurisdiction, U.S.A., 1974, 1976, 1977).

CHAPTER ONE

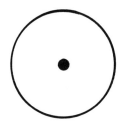

BASIC IDEAS

Few realize that Cabalah developed among the Jews of Egypt and Palestine at a time which saw the true birth of Christianity, or perhaps we should say the monotheistic concept of the God Consciousness. When Moses led the Israelites out of the land of bondage, he carried with him the mysteries of Egyptian knowledge acquired by Moses himself at the court of the Pharaoh. The 19th century French historian and philosopher, Édouard Schuré, makes this doubly clear in his book called *The Great Initiates* when he states:

"Moses, the Egyptian initiate and priest of Osiris, was indisputably the organizer of monotheism. Through him this principle, until then hidden beneath the threefold veil of the Mysteries, came out of the depths of the temple and entered the course of history. Moses had the courage to establish the highest principle of initiation as the sole dogma of a national religion, and the prudence to reveal its consequences to only a small number of initiates, while imposing it upon the masses through fear. In so doing, the prophet of Sinai evidently had before him distant vistas which extended far beyond the destinies of his people. The establishment of the universal religion of mankind is the true mission of Israel, which few Jews other than its greatest prophets have understood."[1]

The Oneness of the Universal Understanding of the God Consciousness is a basic fundamental of not only the Cabalah, but also of many other esoteric philosophies that are being taught around the world today. We find that Moses was trying to establish this concept. Schuré reinforces this thought once more when he says:

"For this undertaking, the most colossal since the prehistoric migration of the Aryans, Moses found an already prepared instrument in the tribes of the Hebrews, particularly in those settled in Egypt in the valley of Goshen, living there in servitude under the name of Beni-Jacob. In the founding of a monotheistic religion he had as forerunners those nomadic and peaceful rulers whom the Bible presents to us in the figures of Abraham, Isaac, and Jacob."[1]

Elsewhere Schuré continues: "A religion is not formed without an initiator. The judges, the prophets, all the history of Israel give proof of Moses; even Jesus himself cannot be conceived without him. Moreover, Genesis contains the essence of the Mosaic tradition. Whatever changes it has undergone, beneath the dust of centuries and priestly wrappings, the venerable mummy must contain the basic idea, the living thought, the testament of the prophet of Israel."[2]

But in spite of its spread to other countries, Cabalah has always remained for the spiritual elite; and frequently, over the last few centuries, it has been lost and rediscovered many times. By the latter part of the 15th century, Spain had become the Cabalistic center of Europe; but then in 1492 the Jews were expelled by Queen Isabella and King Ferdinand, and the Cabalah disappeared from that country. Then during the 16th century the Cabalistic movement arose again and centered in Safed (Safad) in Galilee. And from this center some of the most profound speculative thinkers of their time, such as Moses Cordovero and Isaac Luria, brought forth their teachings. Luria's system of Cabalah affected Jewish piety for generations to come.

The modern Cabalist is heir to a truly ancient doctrine, but he must reinterpret and reformulate this "ever-changing" but always constant cabalistic doctrine so that it is of practical value to him in today's society. Yet he can do this quite easily because much like the *Egyptian Book of the Dead*, and the *Tibetan Book of the Dead*, the Cabalah is a guide book for the soul in its return path upward.

Therefore the saying "Know thyself" is more imperative today than ever before, because the modern-day world is far more complex in this age of anxiety that we live in today. But as man studies himself he finds that he is a miniature of the universe, a microcosm of the macrocosm so to speak, and all that remains is for him to enter the door and use his lamp of light to further guide him in his comprehension of the universe and of himself.

Now what is behind the door, and how does it affect one who has entered it? The noted contemporary philosopher Manly P. Hall explains it in this fashion: "This invisible world is explored only by a few hardy travelers who, striking out from the human race, brave all in their efforts to chart and map the great vistas of eternity. These daring ones are rewarded for their efforts by being accepted into the Invisible. They become citizens of two worlds, and are known as the Initiates and the Masters. Only those who have gradually learned the subtle laws of the invisible nature are permitted to pass beyond the veil."[3]

Yet, the Teachers of many esoteric schools state that it is not nearly as complicated as it might seem, and, in fact, many on the earth plane are passing through that doorway daily. The only drawback is that they are usually not aware of it in their outer consciousness.

We learn that the multiplicity of nature may be studied in order that the student can become aware of the underlying unity behind the diversity of nature. But true esoteric students, surprisingly enough, use the visible only as a means of knowing the invisible. And the invisible is the true reality.

Cabalah is an alphabet of symbols in which a spiritual language is constructed so that communication between Beings in different states of consciousness can be established. In

Cabalah, Gods, angels, and men find a common language. And with Cabalah, we have a tool to explore consciousness from one dimension of experience to another. But the primary task is in grasping the main concepts. Therefore in the following pages of this book will be found the general principles to help unravel the complicated path that leads to the Godhead. And when we understand these principles, we begin to understand the wonders of the Infinite State.

Cabalah could also be said to be a direct penetration into knowledge through comprehension, examination, and meditation. The Bible is being read, and has been read for centuries, but with an understanding contrary to what was originally intended. Then how do we find the true understanding? The answer is through the Cabalah, by learning how to decode a cabalistic text, and by so doing penetrate into an unknown world by means of mathematics and symbols. We need Cabalah to help us understand the true meaning of Scripture.

It is important for the student of the Mysteries to learn to be patient. Insight into the Cabalah evolves slowly. The power of the true mystic begins with reading, learning, meditating, and contemplating; and one cannot follow any better advice than heeding that given by Manly Hall when he states: "Man must cease his efforts to mold the universe according to his own desires, and God's laws to temporal ends. He must realize that he is wise who molds himself into the Divine Plan, and, instead of drawing God and wisdom down to himself, rises through the seven heavens, like Mohammed ascending to the footstool of Divinity."[4]

Religious teaching may be divided into two divisions: (1) the religion of the common man which is called *exoteric* doctrine, and (2) the religion of the wise or the Initiate which is called *esoteric* doctrine. Now one is not any "better" than the other, per se; as each individual will always be attracted to that which he is capable of understanding, and what is right for him at the moment. Yet eventually, in this lifetime or the next, he must arise and accept the higher truths of life. Therefore the esoteric is always cloaked in symbol and ritual to conceal it from those who have not yet reached a certain level of unfoldment. Yet the Cabalah is always available for those who wish to follow the path of the Initiate.

The method of spiritual development must fit the temperament of the aspiring Initiate to be. For a system of spiritual development to work well for those in the West, it must contain certain requirements: It must (1) be easily grasped by Western minds that have little knowledge of mysticism; (2) the forces it unleashes must stimulate the development of the higher aspects of consciousness and be sufficiently powerful to penetrate the minds of Westerners; and (3) the teachings used must make these forces available during the brief periods of time that Western men and women can snatch from their busy daily pursuits. Teachings that are effectual for the recluse of the East are unsatisfactory for the strain of our modern life. The normal, healthy Westerner has no desire to escape from life, his underlying needs being more to conquer life on the earth plane and reduce it to harmony and order. Therefore, the Westerner does not try to escape from matter into spirit; but rather he tries to have the Divine Law prevail in his kingdom.

In order to understand the nature of Being, the Cabalah teaches that there are two great worlds. The higher world is that which is above (the macrocosm); and the lower world is that which is below (the microcosm). Therefore before man can unravel the understanding and nature of God, he must first unravel the mystery of his own Being. But the nature of his microcosmic human consciousness is directly related to the nature of the macrocosmic God Consciousness, and there is no way to truly separate the two. One cannot exist without the other.

It is the great Hermes, in the first two stanzas of his *Precepts of the Emerald Table* who states: "I speak not fictitious things, but that which is certain and True. What is below is like that which is above, and what is above is like that which is below, to accomplish the miracles of one thing."[5]

Cabalists never lost sight of "It is below as it is in Heaven."
The correspondence between the activity of heaven and the
activity of man, or between the macrocosm and the microcosm.

But then in the last two stanzas he reveals the secret by explaining: "And as all things were produced by one word of one Being, so all things were produced from this one thing by *adaptation*. . . . Ascend with the greatest sagacity from the earth to heaven, and then again descend to earth, and unite together the powers of things superior and inferior. Thus you will obtain the glory of the whole world, and obscurity will fly away from you."[6]

Hence, the secret is revealed, and it lies in that one word—*adaptation*. Cabalah gives us the method whereby we can do this, and by the use of symbology and mathematics, we are then able to transform one thing into another. This is the science in which the secret of the Word is known. Man, then, becomes the living magician.

The basic facts are simple: We live between two worlds of existence, and we must learn to live on earth and in heaven at one and the same time. Cabalah uncovers this understanding for us so that we may achieve this state of Being, but the revelation will be given only to those with simplicity of heart and clarity of mind. Only those with the highest motives and the most elevated ideals can hope to gain the true knowledge and wisdom of this science which deals with the secrets of the soul. Others need not apply.

Therefore Cabalah is not merely a body of knowledge in the ordinary sense of the word. It is primarily a method of using the mind in such a way that the Initiate comes into direct contact with the living powers and forces of the Universe, and through them with the eternal source of all manifestation. In other words, you make contact with God.

Now an extensive knowledge of the Hebrew language is most certainly not required of those who wish to study Cabalah. The student will discover that the Cabalah is equally adapted to the English language, and perhaps to many other languages, who can say? For if the words of God are hidden in Scripture, to which "Scripture" should we refer—the Latin, the Hebrew, the English?

The answer will be found in the common denominator of all languages, the Phi principle upon which all things are built. This will be discussed at length in the balance of this book, and there is no need to pursue it further here. But what we should point out is that the decoding of a cabalistic text does not merely involve the transposing of letters to numbers and numbers to letters—which it does—but that it also involves a special manner of *thinking*. This, too, you will discover as you come with us through the balance of the volume.

One concluding thought: The Hebrew word QBLH (Cabalah) is derived from the root word QBL (Qibel), which means "to receive." Therefore, it is hoped that if the reader has the patience to pay close attention to the basic ideas of the Cabalah—including its Tarot, Hebrew, English, and Mathematical aspects which will be explained herewith—he will begin his journey "to receive."

NOTES

1. Édouard Schuré, *The Great Initiates* (U.S.A., Rudolf Steiner Publications, Inc., 1961) pages 172–173.

2. Ibid. *The Great Initiates*, pages 188–189.

3. Manly Palmer Hall, *Collected Writings*, Volume III (Los Angeles, The Philosophical Research Society, Inc., 1962) page 48.

4. Ibid. *Collected Writings*, pages 52–53.

5. The quotation from *Precepts of the Emerald Table of Hermes* is taken from *Kabbalah*, by Charles Ponce (Wheaton, Illinois, The Theosophical Publishing House, 1973) page 142.

6. According to Eliphas Levi, the Emerald Tablet was found by Alexander the Great in the Tomb of Hermes, which was hidden by the priests of Egypt in the depths of the Great Pyramid at Giza. It was supposed to have been written by Hermes on a large plate of emerald by means of a pointed diamond. It is still in existence today, and it is referred to in many early documents, including *L'Alchimie et les Alchimistes*, by Louis Figuier, 7th century, page 42.

CHAPTER TWO

THE INTERCHANGE OF NUMBERS AND LETTERS

he natural meaning of the word "Torah," which stands for the Law books of the Old Testament, is that it is a guide to knowing the proper conduct in life, and it was a proper reading for both Temple and home. But in addition to the obvious meaning, every narrative and verse, and each law, also has a deeper and concealed meaning of a Mystical nature. These can be found by calculation, conversion, and substitution according to the rules of three distinctly different disciplines—Gematria, Notariqon, and Temura. The first name, *Gematria*, was of Greek origin; the second, *Notariqon*, is from the Latin; but the third, *Temura*, was Hebrew, and it meant "permutations" or "changed."

The *Zohar*, the most influential book of Jewish mysticism, says: "If these books of the Torah contain only the tales of, and the words of, Esau, Hagar, Laban, and Balaam, why are they called the Perfect Law, the Law of Truth, and the True Witness of God? There must be a hidden meaning. Woe be to the man who says that the Law (Torah) contains only common sayings and tales: if this were true, we might even in our time compose a book of doctrine which would be more respected."

"No, every word has a sublime sense, and is a heavenly mystery," the text continues. "The Law resembles an angel descending to earth. Just as a spiritual angel must put on a garment to be known or understood here, so the Law must have clothed itself in a garment of words as a body for men to receive; but the wise look within the garments."[1]

Early Cabalists believed that in the Divine words of Scripture, there was a hidden meaning or an essence to be sought out and brought into the light. They believed that God was hidden in these divine Words, and to uncover these hidden meanings the principles of Gematria, Notariqon, and Temura were used as methods of interpretation. The general definitions of the terms are as follows:

(1) GEMATRIA relates to the *numerical values* of words. Words of similar numerical values have a definite relationship with other words with the same number, and they tend to be explanatory of each other.

(2) NOTARIQON relates to *abbreviations*. It literally means quick writing or shorthand, and it is of two forms. The first is where a word is formed from the initial letters of several words; and the second is where the letters of a name become the initial letters of the words in a sentence.

(3) TEMURA relates to *permutations or anagrams*. It consists of an immense variety of rearrangements of the letters in a word to form another word. Sometimes they are even replaced by other letters in accordance with some code.

These concepts have been used in the past in connection with the Hebrew Cabalah; but now we will begin to see how the *English* language is also a "God-given language," and these same general concepts will be used with English. But for the purposes of the English Cabalah, however, we need to derive the numerical values of the English words in a slightly different manner. This new concept is called the *Alpha number* of a word or phrase.

Alpha Number

Any word in the English language may be expressed as a number simply by spelling it, and then adding up the numerical values of each of its letters. In the English Cabalah this is known as the *Alpha number* of the word. Thus A is one, B is two, C is three, etc., all the way up to Z whose number is 26. The Alpha numbers of the various letters of the English alphabet are as follows:

Letter	Alpha Number	Letter	Alpha Number	Letter	Alpha Number
A	1	J	10	S	19
B	2	K	11	T	20
C	3	L	12	U	21
D	4	M	13	V	22
E	5	N	14	W	23
F	6	O	15	X	24
G	7	P	16	Y	25
H	8	Q	17	Z	26
I	9	R	18		

One can see then that the *Alpha number* of a word is *not* the same as the way you would compute it to be in ordinary numerology, wherein the number is reduced to a single digit. The Alpha number is read in its entirety. For example:

GOD = 7 + 15 + 4 = 26   26 is then the Alpha number of GOD,
MAN = 13 + 1 + 14 = 28   and 28 is the Alpha number of MAN

Sometimes you must start with a number, and then deduce its word. For example:

7,154 = 7-15-4 = G + O + D = 26   Thus 7,154 is read as GOD (26),
13,114 = 13-1-14 = M + A + N = 28   and 13,114 is read as MAN (28)

A phrase may be written as a number by inserting a zero (0) in the empty space between the words. Thus:

I LOVE YOU = (9) + 0 + (12-15-22-5) + 0 + (25-15-21)
I LOVE YOU = 9,012,152,250,251,521 (a 16-digit number) or
I LOVE YOU = I (9) + LOVE (54) + YOU (61) = 124

You may also read a number in reverse (remember the Hebrew language is read from right to left).

GOD = 7 + 15 + 4 = 26 = 7,154 or
DOG = 4 + 15 + 7 = 26 = 4,157

In addition to the above, the *digit* zero (0) may also be read as the *letter* O. For example:

The number 704 = 7-0-4 = GOD, or
The number 7,154 = 7-15-4 = GOD

Hence when you come across either one of these numbers (704 or 7,154), you may mentally transform them into the word GOD. The English Cabalah allows for both methods of interpretation.

Gematria (Number Values of Words)

Gematria is the system of deducing the numerical values of words or phrases. *Words of similar numerical values tend to be explanatory of each other.*

At first sight, in some instances, no such relationships may be perceived, but if we persist in our study and meditation, we may come to realize something of the profundities of these subtle connections and associations that are not immediately seen.

Some examples of the method of Gematria follow below (using the English Cabalah and the Alpha numbers of the words).

EARTH = 5 + 1 + 18 + 20 + 8 = 52
DEVIL = 4 + 5 + 22 + 9 + 12 = 52
LIVED = 12 + 9 + 22 + 5 + 4 = 52

Other Gematria examples are as follows:

CROWN = 73   KINGDOM = 73

EXPERIENCE = 104   VORTEX = 104

TAROT = 74   ELEMENT = 74
ENGLISH = 74   CROSS = 74
ENERGY = 74   JESUS = 74

HERMES   =   68   LOGOS = 68
GOD SELF = 26 + 42 = 68   PILLAR = 68
GILGUL = 68 (Hebrew for Reincarnation)

I AM THAT I AM = 9 + 14 + 49 + 9 + 14 = 95
ALMIGHTY   =   95   MILDNESS = 95
THE QUEEN = 33 + 62 = 95   EMPRESS = 95

CHRIST THE KING = 77 + 33 + 41   = 151
JESUS CHRIST = 74 + 77   = 151
HOLY SPIRIT = 60 + 91   = 151
THE GREAT WORK = 33 + 51 + 67   = 151

Isn't it interesting to note that *Jesus Christ* actually is *Christ the King*? since the Alpha numbers of the two terms are identical.

After working with these numbers, you begin to recognize certain words or phrases. For example: When you come across the number 77 (Christ), you always think of the Christ force. But then again, the number 77 is also the Alpha number for the word *Disciple*. It would follow then that the Teacher equates to the student, or balances the vibration, as it were.

It would be a good idea to make your own Gematria dictionary, and thereby have a ready reference for words with similar numerical values.

Notariqon (Abbreviations)

Notariqon is the cabalistic system where abbreviations of words are used to represent the original word. Or sometimes the initial letters of the words in a name will form another word that signifies the whole.

Some examples of Notariqon:

Pr.   = Pair
C.I.A. = Central Intelligence Agency
CA.   = California
U.S.A. = United States of America

The symbols for chemical elements and compounds can also be used:

Au   = Gold
H_2O = Water

Another way to use Notariqon: (and you must use your imagination)

C = Cee   (the name of the letter)
C = Sea   (a large body of water)
C = See   (to observe with the eyes, to comprehend)
C = 3   (the digit 3)

4 = D   (the letter D)
4 = For   (the preposition)
4 = Four   (the name of the digit)

2 = Two   (the name of the digit)
2 = To   (the preposition)
2 = Too   (the adverb)

H = Ache   (the name of the letter, Oxford dictionary)
H = Each   (a rearrangement of the letters, using Temura)

Temura (Permutations, Anagrams)

Temura relates to permutations or anagrams. The letters in any word may be rearranged to make another word, which also tends to explain its meaning. Sometimes the letters are written in a circle, or read backwards. When letters are re-arranged, they will still add up to the same Alpha number.

An example of Temura: Let us take the word TAROT and arrange its letters in a circle in the same manner as the symbol of the serpent swallowing its own tail. Thus the final *T* will occupy the same position on the wheel as the first *T*, symbolizing the conjunction of the beginning and the end. The glyph may then be read in either a clockwise or a counterclockwise direction, thus bringing forth the true meaning for the word TAROT.

ROTA   = Wheel (Latin)
TORA   = Law (Hebrew)
TAROT = The Wheel of the Law

Other examples:

$5\sqrt{5}$ = Five times the square root of five = EVE
$1\sqrt{5}$ = One times the square root of five = AVE,
              which means *Hail* or *Farewell*
DEVIL = 52 = LIVED (when the same word is read in reverse)

ROSE = EROS = The Greek god of love (Cupid), the son of Aphrodite, the goddess of love and beauty

47 = 74 If the number is read from left to right, it is the Alpha number for the word DECIMAL (47); but if we read the same number in reverse, it yields the Alpha number for POINT (74). Thus the Cabalah indicates that the "decimal point" in a number can move in either direction, which it most certainly can.

The Hebrew Numbering System

Inasmuch as the zero (0) was not invented until the third century A.D. by the Arabs, and separate symbols for the digits were not then known, the early Hebrews devised a slightly different numbering system than we use in the English Cabalah of today with its 36 symbols (26 letters + 10 digits).

Yet the Hebrew system was still a *Denary system of numeration:* that is, one that divides its component parts into ones, tens, hundreds, etc., with each letter having a numerical value of exactly 10 times its earlier counterpart. It is the use of the magic of the 10, then, coming some 500 years before the advent of the cipher or the empty space, that makes the Hebrew alphabet so outstanding. The Hebrew letters are shown in the adjacent table, along with their numerical equivalents.

Inasmuch as these 22 letters (or 27 when we consider the Finals) are difficult to write, modern Cabalists have devised a system of substituting an English capital letter, which *sounds* like the original letter, for each letter in the Hebrew alphabet. In this way any Hebrew word can be printed in English with its Hebrew spelling intact, and allow the reader to not only ascertain its numerical value, but also to have a rough idea of the way it is pronounced.

The use of letters to signify numbers was apparently introduced to Palestine during the time of the Second Temple. It never occurred to these early peoples that numbers should be identified any differently. Thus every number became a word, and every word represented a number. However, this system was not unique to the Hebrews; it was also used by the Babylonians and the Greeks.

The first known use of Gematria occurs in an inscription dating back to the time of Sargon II (727–707 B.C.), which says that the king built the wall of Khorsabad 16,283 cubits long to correspond with the numerical value of his name.

Another example of Gematria appears in the Bible in Genesis 18:2, where the words "Lo, three men stood by him" were found by the Hebrew Cabalists to have a numerical value of

PLATE I.—TABLE OF HEBREW AND CHALDEE LETTERS.

Number	Sound or Power.	Hebrew and Chaldee Letters.	Numerical Value.	Roman character by which expressed in this work.	Name.	Signification of Name.
1.	u (soft breathing).	א	1. (Thousands are denoted by a larger letter; thus an Aleph larger than the rest of the letters among which it is, signifies not 1, but 1000.)	**A.**	Aleph.	Ox.
2.	b, bh (v).		2.	**B.**	Beth.	House.
3.	g (hard), gh.		3.	**G.**	Gimel.	Camel.
4.	d, dh (flat th).		4.	**D.**	Daleth.	Door.
5.	h (rough breathing).		5.	**H.**	He.	Window.
6.	v, u, o.		6.	**V.**	Vau.	Peg, nail.
7.	z, dz.		7.	**Z.**	Zayin.	Weapon, sword.
8.	ch (guttural).		8.	**CH.**	Cheth.	Enclosure, fence.
9.	t (strong).		9.	**T.**	Teth.	Serpent.
10.	i, y (as in yes).		10.	**I.**	Yod.	Hand.
11.	k, kh.	Final = ך	20. Final = **500**	**K.**	Caph.	Palm of the hand.
12.	l.		30.	**L.**	Lamed.	Ox-goad.
13.	m.	Final = ם	40. Final = **600**	**M.**	Mem.	Water.
14.	n.	Final = ן	50. Final = **700**	**N.**	Nun.	Fish.
15.	s.		60.	**S.**	Samekh.	Prop, support.
16.	O, aa, ng (gutt.).		70.	**O.**	Ayin.	Eye.
17.	p, ph.	Final = ף	80. Final = **800**	**P.**	Pe.	Mouth.
18.	ts, tz, j.	Final = ץ	90. Final = **900**	**Tz.**	Tzaddi.	Fishing-hook.
19.	q, qh (guttur.).		100. (The finals are not always considered as bearing an increased numerical value.)	**Q.**	Qoph.	Back of the head.
20.	r.		200.	**R.**	Resh.	Head.
21.	sh, s.		300.	**SH.**	Shin.	Tooth.
22.	th, t.		400.	**TH.**	Tau.	Sign of the cross.

The Hebrew Letters with Their English Equivalents According to MacGregor Mathers[2]

701. In the context of the verse, they were easily identified as three of the four archangels, but which ones were they? Simple. They merely added up the values of the names of the arch-angels, and the only ones that would fit were Michael, Gabriel, and Raphael. Therefore, since their names also added up to the same number (701), they were assumed to be the three men referred to.

The Hebrew Cabalists also discovered a deep meaning in each of the Hebrew letters, in their common form as well as their final form; and they found hidden secrets in especially large letters, misplaced letters, and in words spelled in an unusual manner. God was represented at different times by an Aleph (A), or a Yod (I), or a Shin (Sh), or a point within a circle. Sometimes He was represented by a triangle, or a decad of 10 Yods, the exact symbol depending upon the particular aspect of His Consciousness that they were endeavoring to express.

Now let us look at the Temura correspondences. And for that, we must again turn to the Bible. Exodus 3:13–14 reads as follows: "And Moses said unto God, Behold, when I come unto the children of Israel, and shall say unto them, The God of your fathers hath sent me unto you; and they shall say to me, What is his name? what shall I say unto them? And God said unto Moses, I AM THAT I AM . . ." Thus, a relationship is established between *Moses*, the bearer of the Ten Command-ments, and *God*. The Hebrew words and their numerical values are as follows:

MOSES = (M Sh H) = (Mem + Shin + He) = (40 + 300 + 5) = 345
I AM THAT I AM (Ahiye Asher Ahiye)
                    = AHIH AShR AHIH (21 + 501 + 21) = 543

Total Hebrew Numerical Value = 888

When we read the number for MOSES (345) backwards, we bring "I AM THAT I AM" (543) into manifestation. This, then,

seems to explain the strange dialog that went on between
Moses and God in Exodus 33:18–23: "And he (Moses) said, I
beseech thee, show me thy glory . . . And he (God) said, *Thou
canst not see my face:* for there shall no man see me, and live.
And the Lord said, Behold, *there is a place by me,* and thou
shalt stand upon a rock: And it shall come to pass, while my
glory passeth by, that I will put thee in a clift of the rock, and
will cover thee with my hand while I pass by: And I will take
away mine hand, *and thou shalt see my back parts:* but my
face shall not be seen."

We can interpret this to mean that the "back parts" of a
number are its final digits, or the number in reverse, which is
exactly the situation between God and Moses. This relationship is borne out a second time by the way the Hebrew word
for "I AM THAT I AM" is normally spelled in English. The
Alpha numbers are as follows:[3]

$$\begin{aligned}
\text{AHIYE ASHER AHIYE} &= 48 + 51 + 48 = 147 \\
\text{The number in reverse is then:} & \hspace{2em} = 741 \\
\hline
\text{Numerical Sum:} & \hspace{2em} = 888
\end{aligned}$$

Thus we can conclude that the covenant between the God-
Self and the human-self is expressed by the term "I AM THAT
I AM." The beginning digits of the number would be its "face"
(the God-Self); and the final digits of the number would be its
"back parts" (the human-self). Reverse the one, and you have
the other.

The Hebrew/English Cabalah Combined

The very first word in the Bible is the Hebrew word BRAShITh
(Berashith), which means "in the beginning." We all are familiar with the famous phrase, "In the beginning God created the
heaven and the earth (Genesis 1:1)," and this particular Hebrew
word is what starts the process in motion. Let us then examine
it cabalistically and see what we can find.

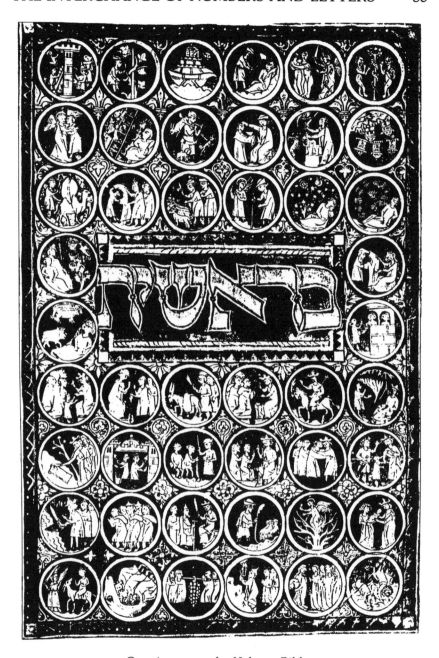

Opening page of a Hebrew Bible.
The Hebrew word BRAShITh (Berashith) meaning "in the beginning"
with a pictorial summary of the biblical narrative (Germany, ca 1300)[4]

Hebrew Letter	Letter Name	Numerical Value
B	Beth	2
R	Resh	200
A	Aleph	1
Sh	Shin	300
I	Yod	10
Th	Taw	400

The Total Hebrew Numerical Value: 913
What the Number Reads in English: I AM (9 + 13)

Here we find, with the aid of the *English* reading of the *Hebrew* numbers, that "In the beginning" (Berashith), I AM. It doesn't seem to make a bit of difference to the "I AM" whether we evaluate His Name by the English Cabalah or the Hebrew Cabalah, for the answer is always the same: I AM. If we go all the way back to the beginning itself, we find that it is not the beginning at all, because this very same "I AM" is already there.

The above is only one example of the many interesting and diverse ways in which the Hebrew Cabalah can be played against the English Cabalah, and quite often with astonishing results. They enhance each other in much the same way as the Yin and the Yang (the passive and active principles of Chinese cosmology), proving once again that the same God Consciousness that designed the one, also designed the other.

There are no hard and fast rules to the potential interchanges and permutations between numbers and letters. The only restrictions imposed upon the seeker as he attempts to interpret the true meaning of a word cabalistically, are the restrictions the seeker imposes upon himself. Your only limitations are the limits of your own ingenuity, as you attempt to solve any given problem. But always remember, that *you must use logic* in your interpretations. The laws of any cabalistic method must always be logical and orderly. Feel free to use your imagination and ingenuity to the utmost as you attempt a cabalistic interpretation of a word. Allow the word to speak to you in the language in which it is trying to express itself, and let it dictate its own rules and reasons for being.

NOTES

1. William Wynn Westcott, *The Kabalah* (England, Percy Lund Humphries & Co. Ltd., The Country Press, 1910, 1926) page 23

2. Taken from *The Kabbalah Unveiled*, by S. L. MacGregor Mathers (London, England, Routledge & Kegan Paul, Ltd., 1887, 1926, 1954) page 3

3. The English spelling for the Hebrew words "Ahiye Asher Ahiye," which mean I AM THAT I AM, are as they appear in *The Secret Doctrine*, Volume 4, by H. P. Blavatsky (India, The Theosophical Publishing House, 1962) page 109

4. Berashith, the first word of the Bible, copied from first page of a Hebrew Bible, Germany, ca 1300, taken from Z'ev ben Shimon Halevi, *Kabbalah* (England, Thames & Hudson, 1979) page 52

5. For additional material on the subject matter of this chapter, the reader is referred to the following books by William Eisen (Marina Del Rey, CA, DeVorss & Co.)

The English Cabalah, Volume I, The Mysteries of Pi (1980)

The English Cabalah, Volume II, The Mysteries of Phi (1982)

The Essence of the Cabalah, (Tarot, Hebrew, English) (1984)

CHAPTER THREE

THE BOOK OF TAROT

The Book of Tarot is a deck of cards, a deck of universal symbols if you will, which if understood in its entirety would be able to express all the laws of Man, God, and the Universe. Its origin is shrouded in mystery. Even though the first physical evidence we have of these cards only goes back to the 14th century, it is the belief of many researchers in the field that at least the general philosophical ideas expressed in the Tarot date back to ancient times.

One of these principles is the biblical idea that "God made man in his own image." Esoteric literature states the same concept in the Hermetic axiom of "as above, so below." Man is the microcosm, the Cosmos in miniature, and by learning more about himself, he will be able to perceive the unity of his internal patterns and those of the Greater Universe of which he is a part.

Eliphas Levi, the early 19th century occultist, was one of the first to combine Tarot and Cabalah into one system. In the frontispiece of his book, *Transcendental Magic*, he shows the great Seal of Solomon, the interlaced double triangles of Macroprosopus and Microprosopus, the two ancients of the Cabalah: the God of Light and the God of Reflections, of mercy and of vengeance, the white Jehovah and the black Jehovah.[1]

"To make light visible," Levi explains, "God had only to postulate shadow." Therefore to manifest the truth, he permitted the possibility of doubt. The shadow (Man) embodies the light, and the possibility of error is essential for the temporal manifestation of truth.

Elsewhere he writes, "The Tarot is a veritable oracle, and replies to all possible questions with precision and infallibility. A prisoner, with no other book than the Tarot, if he knew how to use it, could in a few years acquire a universal science, and would be able to speak on all subjects with unequalled learning and inexhaustible eloquence. The oracles of the Tarot give answers as exact as mathematics, and as measured as the harmonies of Nature. By the aid of these signs and their infinite combinations, it is possible to arrive at the natural and mathematical revelation of all secrets of Nature. The practical value of the Tarot is truly and above all marvelous."

The complete deck of the Tarot consists of 78 individual cards, which are in turn divided into two groups: (1) the Major Arcana or Trump suit expressing 22 universal principles of the God Consciousness, and (2) the Minor Arcana of 56 cards, the forerunner of our modern playing cards, and which expresses the consciousness of Man. Thus from this book our card games have come, but with only vague reminiscences of the earlier use of the mysterious book.

The earlier use, of course, was to preserve, teach, and transmit esoteric philosophy. In these 78 different ideograms, man has been able to learn much about life on the earth plane, and his eventual return to divine perfection. Tarot symbols and numbers are also found in early Bible prophecies. It is said that the Bible is an inspired book, but Tarot is a *book* of inspiration.

Let us begin with the Major Arcana. It consists of 21 num-

As Above, So Below[1]

bered cards plus a zero card, making 22 in all. But the early Hebrew alphabet also contained 22 letters, thus making it possible to make a one-to-one correspondence between the Major Arcana of the Tarot and the Hebrew alphabet. This has been done in the following table, which shows the names of the Tarot cards along with their numbers. We have also included the one key word by which these Trumps may be easily identified; and inasmuch as they really do act as keys to unfoldment, they are usually referred to as Tarot keys.

Hebrew Letter		Tarot No. on Card	Name of Tarot Card	Key Word
Aleph	(A)	1	The Magician	Magician
Beth	(B)	2	The High Priestess	Priestess
Gimel	(G)	3	The Empress	Empress
Daleth	(D)	4	The Emperor	Emperor
He	(H)	5	The Hierophant	Hierophant
Vav	(V)	6	The Lovers	Lovers
Zayin	(Z)	7	The Chariot	Chariot
Cheth	(Ch)	8	Strength	Strength
Teth	(T)	9	The Hermit	Hermit
Yod	(I)	10	The Wheel of Fortune	Wheel
Kaph	(K)	11	Justice	Justice
Lamed	(L)	12	The Hanged Man	Man
Mem	(M)	13	Death	Death
Nun	(N)	14	Temperance	Temperance
Samekh	(S)	15	The Devil	Devil
Ayin	(O)	16	The Tower	Tower
Pe	(P)	17	The Star	Star
Tzaddi	(Tz)	18	The Moon	Moon
Qoph	(Q)	19	The Sun	Sun
Resh	(R)	20	Judgement	Judgement
Shin	(Sh)	0	The Fool	Fool
Taw	(Th)	21	The World	World
22 Letters		231	Sum Total	22 Trumps

Tarot Number

The *Tarot* number of any group of Tarot cards is simply the total value of the numbers as they appear on the cards; and it doesn't make any real difference whether they are being used to build up a word in the Hebrew language, the English language, or any language for that matter, the point being that the Tarot number is always the same for each of the Tarot keys. For example, the Tarot number for the complete Major Arcana is 231 and it never changes. But, if we were to remove the Fool (Tarot Key 0) from the other cards, their value would still be 231 because the Tarot number of the Fool is zero.

Yet we would always "read" a Tarot number as if it were an Alpha number. Therefore the number 231 could be read as the B.C. "A" (Emperor), or, we could read it as (23–1) and state that it stands for the WA(y), the path or course to be traveled from one place to another.

Another interesting point is that the 21 numbered cards can be rearranged in the form of a triangle with the first card, the Magician (Tarot Key 1), occupying the apex position, since 21 is the sum of $(1 + 2 + 3 + 4 + 5 + 6)$. The noted philosopher Manly P. Hall graphically emphasizes this fact by placing all 21 keys of the Major Arcana within the body of the Fool himself. Thus we find that the resulting pyramid represents all of the basic, fundamental forces or ideas that permit you, as an individual, to exist. Each force or card may be considered to be one element or letter of a magical alphabet, the totality of which comprises this pyramid—the Pyramid of Your Own Being.[2]

We have placed the Fool (Tarot Key 0) *in between* Tarot Keys 20 and 21 in the Table of the Major Arcana to emphasize this point: namely, that since his number is 0, he can move anywhere he wishes within his own consciousness in much the same manner as a decimal point moving within the digits of a number. The Major Arcana is his real home. The Fool is only the outer expression of that consciousness. Arthur Edward

The True Meaning of the Fool (Tarot Key 0)
from an Interpretation by Manly P. Hall[2]

Waite (the designer of the Waite or Rider deck of Tarot cards that is used throughout this volume) goes along with this thought; so does Eliphas Levi, Papus and others. Yet other cabalistic groups such as Builders of the Adytum, the Hermetic Order of the Golden Dawn, etc., place the Fool in the 1st Tarot trump position corresponding with the Hebrew letter Aleph, on the premise that the 0 always precedes the number 1. But with the idea that the Fool can move *anywhere* within his own consciousness, the question as to the true location of his abode becomes moot.

Now the Fool (Tarot Key 0) is *You.* And if this Fool, who is you, wishes to know more about the mysteries of his consciousness, he must go on a journey. But before he can do this, he must have some place to go. Therefore the outer worlds are brought into manifestation. These outer worlds that the Fool is about to explore are represented by the four suits of the *Minor Arcana:* Pentacles, Cups, Swords, and Wands. These four kingdoms are analogous to the four basic divisions of Nature: Earth, Water, Air, and Fire, and they go to make up that which is known as Man's outer consciousness. But these kingdoms of his outer consciousness are really nothing more than a *reflection* of his inner consciousness.

The four outer kingdoms of the Tarot are also similar in construction to the Diamonds, Hearts, Spades, and Clubs suits of the modern playing-card deck. Each has ten numbered cards from the Ace to the Ten, but instead of only the Jack, Queen, and King, one extra Court card has been added—the Knight on horseback, bringing the total number of cards in the Minor Arcana up to 56.

We might further add that the four Court cards—the Page, Queen, King, and Knight—represent the royal family and consequently the rulers of each kingdom. The numbered cards represent the major experiences, or the lessons to be learned, that the Fool must encounter as he travels through that particular kingdom. The Ace always represents the beginning of the journey, and the Ten its completion.

Picture Symbols of the Hebrew Alphabet

One can see from the previous discussion that as long as the
Fool (Tarot Key 0) is in motion, and permitted to move *through*
the various elements of the Major Arcana, there is no way to
synchronize the 22 letters of the Hebrew alphabet with the 22
keys of the Major Arcana. Therefore, the allocation of a distinct and unvarying Hebrew letter to each Tarot key is an
impossibility. How then can we identify a permanent picture
symbol with these Hebrew letters?

The answer is simple. In the adjacent table we have retab-
ulated the order number and numerical value of each of the 22
Hebrew letters. The significance of each letter is also shown by
its appropriate symbol. As to when and how these picture
symbols came to be attached to the letters is not known, their
origins being lost in the annals of the past. Yet they do express
the powers and symbolical meanings of these Hebrew letters,
as the following example will show.

Let us examine the word *Cabalah* itself. It is spelled QBLH
in Hebrew, and it is derived from the root word QBL (Qibel),
meaning "to receive." Thus when an H (window) is added,
the word QBLH is the result. Therefore, QBLH (Cabalah) is
defined as being the esoteric Jewish doctrine, which means to
literally *receive* esoteric knowledge through the letter H, the
"window" of the soul (the All-Seeing Eye). And what comes
in through a window? Why Light, of course, and images.

Hebrew Word	Hebrew Letters	Numerical Value	Symbolical Meaning
Q	Qoph	100	Back of Head
B	Beth	2	House
L	Lamed	30	Ox Goad
H	He	5	Window

| Total Sum: | | 137 = MG (Image) | |

The letters within the word QBLH (Cabalah) literally state that its main purpose and function is to *goad* the *house* in the *back of the head* (the brain), so that it may *receive* valuable information and *images* from the pineal gland (the *window* of the soul).

Hebrew Letter		Order Number	Picture Symbol of Hebrew Letter	Numerical Value
Aleph	(A)	1	Ox	1
Beth	(B)	2	House	2
Gimel	(G)	3	Camel	3
Daleth	(D)	4	Door	4
He	(H)	5	Window	5
Vav	(V)	6	Nail, Hook	6
Zayin	(Z)	7	Sword, Armor	7
Cheth	(Ch)	8	Fence	8
Teth	(T)	9	Serpent	9
Yod	(I)	10	Hand	10
Kaph	(K)	11	Palm or Fist	20
Lamed	(L)	12	Ox Goad	30
Mem	(M)	13	Water	40
Nun	(N)	14	Fish	50
Samekh	(S)	15	Prop, Support	60
Ayin	(O)	16	Eye, Anger	70
Pe	(P)	17	Mouth	80
Tzaddi	(Tz)	18	Fish-hook	90
Qoph	(Q)	19	Back of Head	100
Resh	(R)	20	Head	200
Shin	(Sh)	21	Tooth	300
Taw	(Th)	22	Cross	400
22 Letters		253	Sum Total	1,495
BE C				A DIE

Picture Symbols of the English Alphabet

Now let us look at the English Alphabet. What is the meaning of the letter A, the letter B, the letter C? Is there a picture
symbol associated with each of the 26 letters of the English
alphabet, in the same way that there was with the Hebrew
alphabet? If the letters of the Hebrew alphabet had their own
individual symbols, why then doesn't the English alphabet
have its own set of symbols? It would be reasonable to assume
that it does, and if there is such a thing as an English Cabalah,
the only thing remaining is to seek them out.

But we don't have to look very far for our answer, because
just about the same time that the English alphabet was being
finalized with the additions of the letters J and W to the 24-
letter Latin alphabet (around the 11th century A.D.), the Book
of Tarot was more than likely making its appearance, although
we don't have any physical evidence of it until the 14th century. Though there is a relationship between the 22 letters of
the Hebrew alphabet and the 22 keys of the Major Arcana,
the true symbology of the Tarot must rest with a more modern
alphabet because of the very great age differential between
the two systems (the Tarot and the Hebrew). And what is the
most likely candidate? The obvious answer is the English
alphabet, the alphabet of one of the most universal languages
in the world today—English.

There are really 26 picture symbols in the Book of Tarot
when we take the four Court cards, the Page, Queen, King,
and Knight into consideration. When we add these four symbols of the Minor Arcana to the 22 Tarot keys of the Major
Arcana, we could theoretically make a one-to-one correspondence with the 26 letters of the English alphabet.

Several have tried to make these correspondences, including
William Gray in *The Talking Tree* (1977),[3] and others, but it
seems that William Eisen was the first one to do it successfully
in Volume I of *The English Cabalah* (1980).[4] He says that it

took seven years for the process to unfold itself (from 1971 to 1978, when the final match was consummated), and the correct English-to-Tarot correspondences are tabulated in the following table.

English Letter	Alpha Number	Name of Tarot Card	Tarot Number	Key Word Alpha Number	Card Name Alpha Number
A	1	The *Emperor*	4	90	123
B	2	The *Wheel* of Fortune	10	53	206
C	3	The *Moon*	18	57	90
D	4	The *Devil*	15	52	85
E	5	The *Hierophant*	5	114	147
F	6	The High *Priestess*	2	130	195
G	7	*Justice*	11	87	87
H	8	The *Hermit*	9	73	106
I	9	The *Magician*	1	57	90
J	10	The *World*	21	72	105
K	11	The *King*	11	41	74
L	12	The *Knight*	12	69	102
M	13	*Death*	13	38	38
N	14	The Hanged *Man*	12	28	100
O	15	The *Sun*	19	54	87
P	16	The *Page*	16	29	62
Q	17	The *Queen*	17	62	95
R	18	The *Tower*	16	81	114
S	19	The *Star*	17	58	91
T	20	*Temperance*	14	100	100
U	21	The *Fool*	0	48	81
V	22	The *Lovers*	6	91	124
W	23	The *Chariot*	7	74	107
X	24	*Judgement*	20	99	99
Y	25	*Strength*	8	111	111
Z	26	The *Empress*	3	95	128
26 Letters	351	Sum Total	287	1,863	2,747

Seven Examples of the Interchange between Alpha and Tarot

Before we get into examples of the interchange between the Tarot cards and the English letter symbols with which they are identified, a further explanation of this table of correspondences is in order.

1. The names of the Tarot cards appearing in the table are identical to those used by Arthur Edward Waite in *The Pictorial Key to the Tarot* (first published in 1910), and also on the cards themselves of his deck. The Waite deck of cards is called "The Rider Tarot Deck," and is by far the most popular and has become almost a standard throughout the English-speaking world today.[5]

2. The underlined words in the Tarot names are the key words by which they are identified. The full *name* of Tarot Key 10 is "The Wheel of Fortune," the Alpha number of which is 206; but its key *word* is simply "Wheel," with an Alpha number of 53. Now since this Tarot card is identified with the English letter B, the second letter of the English alphabet, the *Alpha* number of the card itself is 2, as opposed to its *Tarot* number which is 10; and it always shall remain 10 since the two systems, while interrelated, are still independent of each other.

3. *Tarot* number for any word or phrase is simply the total value of the *Tarot* numbers of the letters making up the word. Therefore the *Tarot* number of GOD is 45 (11 + 19 + 15); as opposed to its *Alpha* number which is 26 (7 + 15 + 4). Yet a Tarot number is still *read* in the same way that you would read any number, it making no real difference how the number was originally derived. For example: the *symbol* for the Moon (Tarot Key 18) is the English letter C; but its *Tarot card* number is 18, and it would be read as R (18) or AH (1 + 8).

4. The *Tarot* numbers for the four Court cards—the King, Knight, Page, and Queen—even though there are no numbers appearing on the cards, are also the same as their *Alpha* numbers. The reason for this is that the Minor Arcana of the Tarot is the common denominator for *both* the Alpha and the Tarot systems of numeration.

Example 1

Now does the system work? By that, I mean does the combination of the Alpha number system of the English Cabalah, when combined with the numbering system of the Tarot, actually produce valid results? Well, we will let you the reader be the judge of that, but as far as we can determine, the English language does indeed become the key that unlocks the real meaning of number, Tarotwise and Alphawise. Therefore, let us use the word CABALAH itself as our first example. There are four sets of numbers we can use: (1) Card Alpha number, (2) Card Tarot number (3) Key Word Alpha number, (4) Card Name Alpha number. The numbers are tabulated below:

Name of Tarot Card	Letter Symbol	CARD Alpha Number	CARD Tarot Number	KEY WORD Alpha Number	CARD NAME Alpha Number
The *Moon*	C	3	18	57	90
The *Emperor*	A	1	4	90	123
The *Wheel* of Fortune	B	2	10	53	206
The *Emperor*	A	1	4	90	123
The *Knight*	L	12	12	69	102
The *Emperor*	A	1	4	90	123
The *Hermit*	H	8	9	73	106
Sum Total:		28	61	522	873
		MAN	YOU	E V	H H

Man

THE HANGED MAN.

Whenever you come across the same number as the Alpha number of either the *key word* or the *name* of a Tarot card, the Cabalah permits you to substitute its appropriate letter for that number. Therefore, since the Alpha number of CABA-LAH is 28, we can say that it equates to MAN (28). And since its Tarot number is 61, which is the same as YOU (61), we can more or less say that it equates to the HUMAN.

This is verified by the Alpha number total of the key words (522), which may be read as EVe, the first woman; and the Alpha number total of the card names (873), which furnishes us with a pair of H's (73 = Hermit = H) to complete the words that make up "H (Each) H–U–MAN."

Example 2

The Tarot card for JUSTICE (Tarot Key 11) pictures a female figure seated between two pillars. She holds a sword in her right hand symbolizing her potential severity, and a pair of scales in her left hand showing balanced judgment. Normally she is blindfolded, but in the Tarot deck her eyes are unveiled, symbolizing Divine Justice at work rather than the blindness of human justice.

These are the meanings we can glean from a simple observation of the card, but what are its deeper meanings? What does the word JUSTICE itself have to say? We can find out by performing a cabalistic analysis similar to the previous one, and to our absolute astonishment and amazement, we find that the total Alpha value of the Tarot cards representing the letters in its name equates to GOD!

$$JUSTICE = 704 = GOD$$

The reader can satisfy himself as to the validity of our analysis by studying the tabulation of the four sets of numbers for the word JUSTICE that appears on the following page. The results are nothing less than incredible.

The Elements of JUSTICE.

Name of Tarot Card	Letter Symbol	CARD Alpha Number	CARD Tarot Number	KEY WORD Alpha Number	CARD NAME Alpha Number
The *World*	J	10	21	72	105
The *Fool*	U	21	0	48	81
The *Star*	S	19	17	58	91
Temperance	T	20	14	100	100
The *Magician*	I	9	1	57	90
The *Moon*	C	3	18	57	90
The *Hierophant*	E	5	5	114	147
Sum Total:		87	76	506	704
	THE SUN = O	GF		EOF (FOE)	GOD

It is also interesting to note that the letter G, the symbol for JUSTICE (Tarot Key 11), appears near the entrance to every Masonic lodge (in the space between the compass and the square). And what does it represent? Some say GEOMETRY, but many have come to the realization that it stands for GOD. Both are correct, and the Cabalah furnishes us with the proof.

But the letter G is not its only symbol. An alternate symbol is the two pans of a pair of scales, with the forces of GOD on the one hand balancing the forces of his FOE (the Devil) on the other. This, too, is demonstrated in the above tabulation, when the sum of the values of the key words for JUSTICE (506) are read from right to left (FOE).

Furthermore, the Alpha number for THE SUN (Tarot Key 19), the English letter O, is the same as that of JUSTICE (87). Therefore the Cabalah also shows us that the Sun is an effigy (FG) of the E (Energy) OF GOD!

Example 3

Have you ever wondered just exactly what GOD might look like? Many esoteric schools of philosophy have always taught

JUSTICE

DEVIL

D

SUN

O

JUSTICE

G

that the only "God" you will ever know is your individual concept of Him. But perhaps there is a better way, and that is to create a picture of the Word itself. This has been done in the figure on the adjacent page.

The first thing that I hear you exclaim is: "The Devil, what is he doing in the word GOD?" And on the surface, this sounds like a very reasonable question. But now let us think about it for a moment. One of the basic and most fundamental concepts of the meaning of the Universal Consciousness of God is that it represents *all there is.* Not a part of it, but the entire whole. That is why the God Consciousness is usually represented in the Cabalah as the ONENESS. And if God is One, the complete whole, there is certainly no room for the Devil, or the Anti-God, to be outside of it.

God is therefore positive as well as negative, justice as well as injustice, one being weighed against the other in the two pans of the scales which are in balance about the fulcrum, the center of the solar system symbolized by the Sun (Tarot Key 19), the letter O. Positive, Negative, and Neutral: that is the picture of the God Consciousness.

Or, another phrase used many times to describe the God Consciousness is the simple statement, "I AM." And again, we have further confirmation of this fact from a simple cabalistic analysis of the names of the three Tarot cards making up the one word GOD:

Letter Symbol	Name of Tarot Card	Alpha Number
G	JUSTICE	87
O	THE SUN	87
D	THE DEVIL	85
	Sum Total:	259
		BE I

Doesn't "I AM" mean the same thing as "BE I"?

Moon

Example 4

The symbol for the Tarot card for THE MOON (Tarot Key 18) is the crescent, the letter C, the third letter of the English alphabet. It furnishes the power so that life may evolve from out of the *sea* (the C) and onto the shore. The way of evolution upon the earth plane is very clearly marked, and it is symbolized by a long, winding path that leads from the sea and across the land. About halfway up the path are two pillars or towers, and it eventually ascends into the rugged mountains in the distance.

But the symbol "*c*" is also the scientific symbol for the velocity of *Light* (the electromagnetic constant), and which is equal to 300,000 kilometers per second, again a manifestation of the number 3. Let us then analyze the word LIGHT, and see if we can trace it back to the orthodox symbology reflected on the Tarot card.

We will begin with the number formed by the natural sequence of the letters in a word or phrase. And when we do this, we will find an absolutely astounding confirmation of the relationships between the two systems of symbology.

$$\text{LIGHT} = \begin{matrix} 12\,9\ \ 7\ \ 8\,20 \\ \text{L I G H T} \end{matrix} = \begin{matrix} 1{,}297{,}820 \\ \text{A BIG } H_2O \end{matrix}$$

This is most revealing inasmuch as H_2O is the chemical symbol for Water, and not only that, but a BIG WATER is a SEA, which in turn may be changed to CEE, the name of the letter "C." Thus through the magic of Cabalah, we finally learn just why the word LIGHT is spelled the way it is, proving once again that the real power of the English language lies in the spelling of its words, and not necessarily in the way they are pronounced.

Therefore, as we now gaze at the Moon in the LIGHT of our new understanding, we can clearly SEE why life must evolve from out of the SEA and into the CEE. Everywhere we look, it

DEATH

M

would seem, there is amazing confirmation of the hidden wisdom contained within the Cabalah.

Example 5

A mysterious rider on a white horse moves slowly, bearing a black banner emblazoned with a five-petaled mystic white rose. Although he is suited up in black armor with a black helmet and red plume, the horseman carries no visible weapon. Yet king, child, and maiden fall before him, while a bishop with clasped hands awaits the release of his mortal consciousness from earthly living.

The symbol for DEATH (Tarot Key 13) is the letter M, and it is interesting to observe that if one will recite the alphabet out loud from A to Z, the mouth will remain open at the sound of every letter except the M. Here, the lips will remain very tightly closed, as if to signify Death—and Silence.

But rebirth and renewal is the true keynote of this card, because in the distance, between two towers or pillars on the edge of the horizon, shines the sun of immortality. The moment it sets in one hemisphere it rises in the other, causing but a momentary lapse in consciousness. Life is therefore supported by its continual motion—birth, death, and then its constant renewal—proving once more that the process of disintegration is for the sole purpose of the release of energy.

The Cabalah very explicitly points this out, because the letter M is the *only* letter that is universally the same in its Tarot aspect, its Hebrew aspect, and its English aspect:

13th Tarot key = Death   = M
13th Hebrew letter = Mem = M
13th English letter   = M

It would naturally follow that if we are to understand the true meaning of this card, we must first remove a few veils from the mysterious number 13. And how do we do this? The reader is invited to turn the page and find out.

JUDGEMENT

The cabalistic solution to a problem such as this always lies in discovering the appropriate *transformation*, and in this particular instance it is found in converting the number 13 into its equivalent word. The Alpha number for the *word* THIRTEEN is found to be 99, the same as the number for JUDGEMENT (Tarot Key 20), whose symbol is the letter X, the same as the Greek letter Chi, and the symbol for Christ (Xmas, etc.).

Here, the dead are shown arising from their coffins in great wonderment, adoration, and ecstasy as the angel Gabriel emerges out of the clouds blowing on his trumpet. The coffins float on the great sea of cosmic mind that separates the lower physical plane from the higher spiritual levels of consciousness; yet they have not yet reached the ultimate since the snow-capped peaks in the distance indicate the need for still further attainment.

But even so, we can still conclude that the rider on the white horse, with each of his measured steps, brings to the recipient not Death—but Life.

Example 6

"And the Lord God caused a deep sleep to fall upon Adam, and he slept: and he took one of his ribs, and closed up the flesh instead thereof; And the rib, which the lord God had taken from man, made he a woman, and brought her unto the man." (Genesis 2:21–22). Thus the Bible states that Eve was created through and by the removal of a rib from Adam.

Impossible, you say? No, not at all. The biblical creation of Eve is based upon strict, cabalistic principles: You start with the symbol for Adam which is A, then you invert it to change its polarity from positive to negative, and you complete the process by removing the central "rib" from the A and lo—there stands the symbol for Eve, the letter V.

"But the first initial for the word *Eve* is E," you reply. True, but the letter V also stands for Eve since the word *Eve* is really an anagram for *Vee*, the name of the letter whose symbol is V.

LOVERS

Therefore, V = VEE = EVE. We find that THE LOVERS (Tarot Key 6), even though it represents the two of them, Adam as well as Eve, may also be used to designate the feminine principle only.

Now who are Adam and Eve? They are the male and female counterparts of the one soul. They are you and your soul mate, the hero and heroine of your own individual life drama. They are the twin souls or the "double you." Their Alpha numbers bear this out. Thus: YOU AND I = (61 + 19 + 9) = 89, are the many "ADAM AND EVES," which also equal 89 or "Each I" (19 + 19 + 51 = 89). Even the Alpha number for ADAM (19), when combined with that for EVE (32), adds up to 51 which may be read as EA., the abbreviation for *Each*.

One final thought:

```
EVE LOVES ADAM = 32 + 73 + 19 = 124 = THE LOVERS (33 + 91)
ADAM LOVES EVE = 19 + 73 + 32 = 124 = THE LOVERS (33 + 91)
      I LOVE YOU =  9 + 54 + 61 = 124 = THE LOVERS (33 + 91)
```

In the final analysis it would then seem that LOVE, whose Alpha number is the same as SUN (54), is the one Force around which the world revolves.

Example 7

The Tarot card for THE WORLD (Tarot Key 21) is a beautiful example of one of the most basic principles of the Cabalah. "What is that?" you ask. Well, let us study this Tarot card and try to find out just what it is that it represents. But we don't have to look very long for our answer, for its four kingdoms are very clearly identified at the four corners of the card.

They turn out to be the four mystical Living Creatures seen by the prophet Ezekiel in his vision (the Bull, the Lion, the Eagle, and Man), representing the four fixed signs of the Zodiac. Yet, in the final analysis, they become integral parts of the great ONENESS that embraces all things.

WORLD

For example: the four kingdoms of the Minor Arcana are Cups, Swords, Pentacles, and Wands, with Alpha numbers of 59, 98, 95, and 61, respectively. And the Alpha numbers for Man, Bull, Lion, and Eagle are 28, 47, 50, and 30. Now this in itself is not too unusual, but when we combine Cups with Man, Swords with Bull, Pentacles with Lion, and Wands with Eagle, the results are astonishing! It would appear that the Universal God Consciousness chose the English names for these four kingdoms with the utmost precision, for by simply reading the Alpha numbers around the World in the order named, we find that we bring the ONENESS into manifestation once again.

MAN	28
CUPS	59
THE SUN	= 87

O

EAGLE	30
WANDS	61
THE STAR	= 91

S

| ONENESS | = 91 |

S

BULL	47
SWORDS	98
Total	= 145

N E

THE WORLD.

LION	50
PENTACLES	95
Total	= 145

N E

The Great Oneness of All Things

NOTES

1. Eliphas Levi, *Transcendental Magic* (London, William Rider and Son, 1923) opposite page 1

2. The pyramid drawing of the Major Arcana is from *The Secret Teachings of All Ages*, by Manly Palmer Hall, An Analysis of the Tarot Cards (Los Angeles, The Philosophical Research Society, Inc., 1928, 1978) page CXXIX

3. William Gray, *The Talking Tree* (York Beach, Maine, Samuel Weiser, Inc., 1977)

4. William Eisen, *The English Cabalah*, Volume I, The Mysteries of Pi (Marina Del Rey, CA., DeVorss and Company, 1980)

5. Arthur Edward Waite, *Pictorial Key to the Tarot* (New York, University Books, 1910, 1959). The Tarot card illustrations that we are using in this chapter are from the Waite deck, but since it was first published by William Rider & Son, Ltd., it is sometimes called the Rider deck.

CHAPTER FOUR

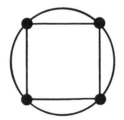

THE MATHEMATICS OF CABALAH,
THE PHI PRINCIPLE

In this volume it is of paramount importance to point out to the student of Cabalah how the principle of *Phi pervades our physical universe.* As demonstrated in this chapter, the reader will discover how both *Nature and man himself are constructed on this principle.* Then most certainly Cabalah, which is our map to understanding the laws of the universe and of man, must also take Phi into consideration. Therefore in the following pages we will explore the principles of Phi.

In William Eisen's books on Cabalah he clearly shows how mathematics is a most important part of Cabalah. All mathematics are used in its construction, including the great principles of Pi (π), Phi (ϕ), e (the base of natural logarithms), and i ($\sqrt{-1}$), but in *Cabalah Primer* we introduce only the most significant principle: Phi, the great principle of the Golden Mean.

Cabalah makes us think and work. Nothing of value is learned without duress. Some students will find this chapter a little more difficult because here we deal with mathematics; don't be discouraged, you may want to return to this material later. Symbols and numbers are important principles of Cabalah which take perseverance and effort to master. For those who are ready, the mathematical principles studied here will be well worth the effort.

As Eliphas Levi, the 19th century occultist, reminds us in *The Book of Splendours:* "Characteristics necessary to success in this study (Cabalah) are a great rectitude of judgment and a great independence of mind. One must rid oneself of all prejudice and every preconceived notion, and it is for this reason that Christ said, 'Unless you become as a little child, you cannot enter into the kingdom of knowledge'."

The Divine Proportion

Geometry has two great treasures: one is the theorem of Pythagoras; the other, the division of a line into extreme and mean ratio. The first we may compare to a measure of gold; the second we may name a precious jewel.
                           —Johannes Kepler (1571–1630)

In ancient Greece, the most famous of all axioms about proportion was that for maximum aesthetic appeal, a line should be divided into two *unequal* parts in such a way that the lesser is to the greater as the greater is to the whole. This was called the Golden Section, the Golden Cut, the division of a line proportionally into mean and extreme ratio. This emphasis upon the correct interrelationship of the parts to the whole prevailed throughout the entire Classical period. This "Divine Proportion" later came to be called the *Golden Mean*, eventually ending up with the 21st letter of the Greek alphabet ϕ (Phi) as its symbol.

$$\overline{\quad\overset{\displaystyle\cdot}{A}\qquad\qquad\overset{\displaystyle\cdot}{B}\qquad\qquad\qquad\overset{\displaystyle\cdot}{C}\quad}$$

The Golden Cut, or Divine Proportion, is represented as the exact ratio in which the line AC can be divided by the point B, whereby the ratio between BC and AB is in a true Phi proportion. Thus:

$$\frac{BC}{AB} = \frac{AC}{BC} = \text{Phi} = \phi = 1.618 \ldots$$

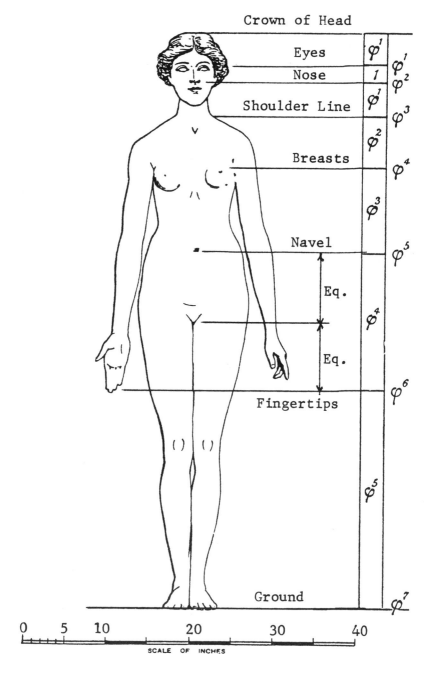

The Phi Pattern in the Human Form[1]

In the terminology of the early mathematicians, this meant dividing the line AC into "extreme and mean ratio." It was later called the "Divine Proportion" by Kepler.

There seems to be little doubt that the Greek architects and sculptors incorporated this Phi ratio in their artifacts. Phidias, the most famous Greek sculptor of the fifth century BC, made use of it. It was Phidias who directed the construction of the Parthenon, and the proportions of its facade illustrate this point.

In the following figure:

$$\frac{b}{a} = \frac{c}{b} = \frac{d}{c} = \frac{e}{d} = \frac{f}{e} = \frac{\phi}{1} = 1.618 \ldots = \text{Phi}.$$

It is also to be noted that $(a + b = c)$, $(b + c = d)$, $(c + d = e)$, etc. It is quite evident that the overall width of the facade should be taken at the entablature, and not at the bottom of the steps, as it was assumed to be in the earlier drawing.

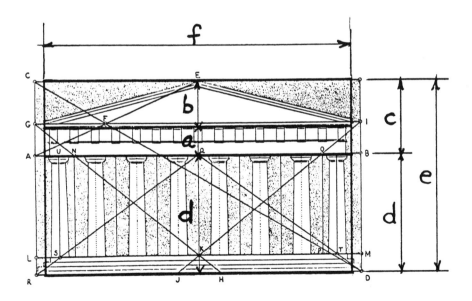

The Phi Pattern in the Facade of the Parthenon[2]

Fibonacci Numbers

Man has learned to count by using the numbers 0, 1, 2, 3, 4, 5, 6, 7, 8, 9, 10, etc. All things begin with the zero (0) to represent the starting point from which they are measured. But Nature would count them differently. The system she would use would be the numbers 0, 1, 1, 2, 3, 5, 8, 13, 21, 34, 55 . . . , of which the first two numbers are 0 and 1, and *each succeeding number is the sum of the two immediately preceding it.* These are called Fibonacci numbers in honor of the man who first discovered them, Leonardo Fibonacci, the most distinguished mathematician of the Middle Ages.

The Fibonacci numbering system is applicable, although sometimes in a modified form, to the growth of every living thing, and it makes no difference whether it is a single cell, a grain of wheat, a hive of bees, or even Man himself. This may come as a surprise to the average reader, but nevertheless if you pursue your studies of the laws of Phi you will find that it is so.

As the numbers in the Fibonacci sequence increase in magnitude, the ratio between adjacent terms approaches closer and closer to this Golden Number: Phi, the Divine Proportion, the great Golden Mean of the Greeks. Its value is expressed algebraically as follows:

$$\text{Phi} = \phi = \frac{1 + \sqrt{5}}{2} = 1.618033 \ldots$$

However, no matter how many terms in the Fibonacci sequence we analyze, the number Phi is never reached but only approximated. The ratio between two succeeding terms always alternates from a little higher to a little lower than the Golden Number.

To achieve exact quantities of this infinitely long decimal we must add what is known as the Lucas numbers, but in this primer we will deal only with Fibonacci numbers. When the student wants to go beyond the primer, he will have to pursue some of the more advanced books on the Cabalah which delve into the Phi laws to a much greater extent; but for the moment, the Fibonacci numbers will be sufficient to explain them.

The following chart involving the procreation of rabbits illustrates the Fibonacci sequence of numbers as they appear in nature:

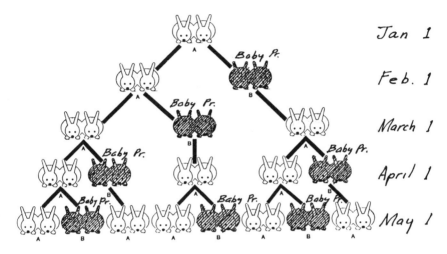

A Chart of the Procreation of Rabbits[3]

Let us say that a man puts a single pair of rabbits in a pen enclosed on all sides by a wall. The question: How many pairs of rabbits can be produced from the original pair in the course of one year if it is assumed that every month each pair begets another pair, and that all new rabbits begin to bear young two months after their own birth?

Therefore on January 1 there is only an adult pair of rabbits. On February 1 there are the original adults and a new baby pair. On March 1 the baby pair has now grown to maturity, making two adult pairs as well as a new baby pair produced by the original pair. The process will continue in this manner until the following January 1, when it is seen from the table that there will be 377 pairs of rabbits in the pen including the original pair who are presumed to be still alive and well. Thus we are introduced to the tremendous procreative ability of Nature.

Date	Number of Adult Pairs	Number of Baby Pairs	Total Number of Pairs
January 1	1	0	1
February 1	1	1	2
March 1	2	1	3
April 1	3	2	5
May 1	5	3	8
June 1	8	5	13
July 1	13	8	21
August 1	21	13	34
September 1	34	21	55
October 1	55	34	89
November 1	89	55	144
December 1	144	89	233
January 1	233	144	377

All of the numbers in the above table are Fibonacci numbers, Nature's own numbering system, which is formed according to the rule that *any term in the series is the sum of the two preceding terms.* This fascinating series is all important because it is an essential component of the mathematical laws governing growth and reproduction.

Perhaps the most spectacular manifestation of Nature's Golden Numbers is observed in the pattern of the florets of the common daisy, the bracts of a pinecone, the scales of a pineapple, and the seeds within the flowering head of a giant sunflower. Within each of these somewhat different species, a remarkable similarity exists. That similarity is that they all contain two sets of spirals, concurrent and intertwined with each other, and yet running in opposite directions.

The particular species of pinecone in the above illustration displays 8 spirals running in one direction and 13 spirals in the other, both of them being Fibonacci numbers. One is a right-hand spiral and the other a left-hand spiral, with the net result that each bract (the tab-like leaf of the pinecone) fulfills a dual role by belonging to two different spirals at one and the same time.

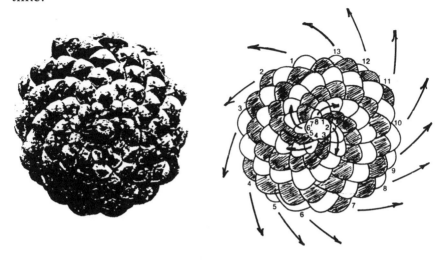

The Spiral Arrangement of the Bracts of a Pinecone[4]

This alone is interesting enough, but what is so fascinating about the combination is that the number of spirals in each system is *always an adjacent Fibonacci number.* One species might be composed of the numbers 5 and 8, another with the numbers 8 and 13, but *the result is always a Fibonacci combination.* One investigation of 4,290 pinecones, randomly taken from ten different species of pine found in California, showed that only 74 cones (1.7% of the total) deviated from the Fibonacci pattern. Thus while these patterns are quite obviously not an inviolable law of Mother Nature, they are most certainly curiously persistent.

The Pentagram

One cannot begin to understand the magical qualities of the pentagram without also embracing its counterpart the pentagon. It is unfortunate that the two terms sound so very much alike, but there is nothing we can do about it because these are their names. Yet when we observe the two figures, one within the other, all confusion vanishes once we understand their true relationship. The following figure tries to bring this about, but a further clarification seems to be necessary.

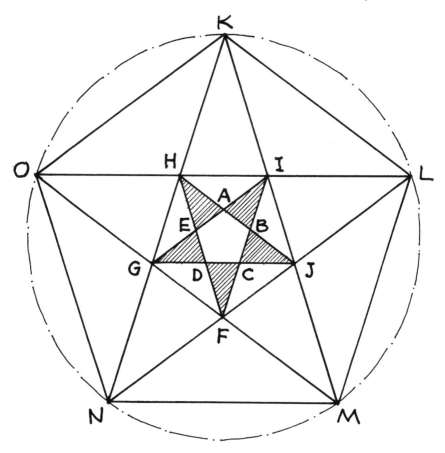

Let us look at it this way: Way back in the beginning of time, eons and eons ago, was the undeveloped bud of a flower. Let us call it a rosebud, and let us say it was in the shape of a pentagon. Let us further say that it is the pentagon A–B–C–D–E in the preceding figure. Its petals are folded inwards along the perimeter, but eventually comes the time for it to blossom. Then, suddenly, the shaded petals unfold and swing open, and the 5-petaled pentagram *F–G–H–I–J* is the result. This same process is continued over and over again, with each successive flower becoming larger and larger and larger, until the universe itself is in the shape of a beautiful garden.

This is the soul; this is man; this is You. Man is in the process of unfolding in much the same way as the rose in the previous figure, and this entire process can be measured as precisely as any other force in nature. This is one of the reasons the Rosicrucian Brotherhood chose for its symbol the Rosy Cross, the rose unfolding and blossoming on the cross of matter.

Now let us give a thought to the two different types of five-pointed stars or pentacles that unfold from any central pentagon. We use the word "pentacles" to denote the plural of the *pentagram* in order to keep the numerical vibrations of the term intact:

Name of Term	Number of Words	Number of Letters	Alpha Number
PENTAGRAM	1	9	95
PENTACLES	1	9	95

Here we find that the one is equal to the many, that the numerical vibrations of the all-inclusive word "Pentagram" are equal in every respect to the infinite number of "Pentacles" folded up within it.

Now that we have a general idea of the basic symbology of the Pentagram, let us try to ascertain the secret of its power. Earlier, we learned of the great power of Phi, the Golden Mean, the invisible influence that is forever present within all things. And the Pentagram, as the reader is about to see, is a veritable treasure trove of golden ratios, as proven by the diagram on the following page.

This figure is really no different from the previous one, the only difference being that the Soul of the Pentagram is now laid bare for all to see. The Golden Isosceles Triangle that makes up the upper petal of the rose, or star as we shall now

call it, has been further subdivided into smaller and smaller
pentagons as we project ourselves up to the apex point.

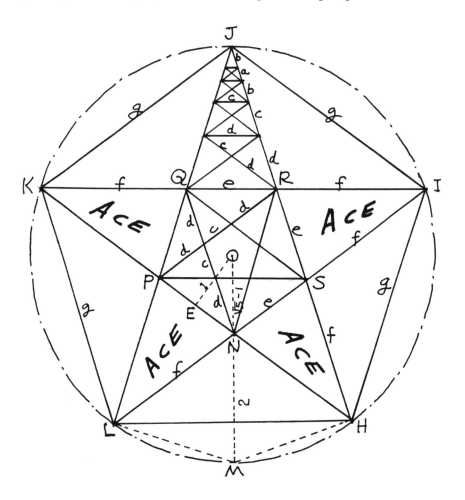

The Internal Structure within the Pentagram

Actually, the apex is never reached, as the number of pentagons between the center of the circle (O) and the apex (J) are
infinite in number. This is because each division of a Golden
Isosceles Triangle (the petal of the star), in much the same way
as the facade of the Parthenon, or even the human form itself,

becomes a separate term in the Phi sequence of numbers. Each term is designated by a lower-case letter in the same way that we identified the various divisions of the Parthenon; that is, consecutive terms in the Phi series of numbers are identified by consecutive letters. Thus:

$$\frac{b}{a} = \frac{c}{b} = \frac{d}{c} = \frac{e}{d} = \frac{f}{e} = \frac{g}{f} = \frac{\phi}{1} = 1.618033 \ldots = \text{Phi}$$

Moreover:

$$(a + b = c), (b + c = d), (c + d = e),$$
etc., on and on—forever

Now let us look at our Pentagram in still another way. Actually, it can easily be seen that a Pentagram is really nothing more than five capital A's, placed one above the other in a circle, and rotated so that their apexes are at equal distances along the circumference. This then gives us five kingdoms or "Aces" abutting a central, pentagon-shaped core. And there is nothing stopping us from dividing each one of these five kingdoms in the same manner that we did with the upper part of the star. Now does the reader see anything unusual or significant here? There certainly is, because the Tarot deck is represented in its entirety. The Aces of each one of the four suits of the Minor Arcana (Swords, Wands, Cups, and Pentacles) occupy the four lower parts of the Pentagram, and the uppermost part, the spiritual part, is occupied by the Emperor himself, the letter A, representing the Trump suit of the Major Arcana. And who is in the central, pentagon-shaped core? The Fool (Tarot Key 0), of course, whose symbol is U, and whose name is *You*.

The allegorical Star of the Magi is then the mysterious Pentagram; and those three kings, sons of Zoroaster who were conducted by the Blazing Star to the cradle of the microcosmic God, are themselves a full demonstration of the cabalistic and magical beginnings of Christian doctrine. Eliphas Levi states that "one of these kings is white, another black, and the third brown. The white king offers gold, symbol of light and life;

the black king presents myrrh, image of death and darkness; the brown king sacrifices incense, emblem of the conciliating doctrine of the two principles. They return thereafter into their own land by another road, to show that a new cultus is only a new path, conducting man to one religion, being that of the sacred triad and the radiant Pentagram."[5] Thus according to Levi, all symbols of occultism are summed up in the sign of the Pentagram, which Paracelsus proclaims to be the greatest and most potent of all signs.

The Pentagram: Symbol of Man[6]

And the reason that the Pentagram is the greatest and most potent of all the signs is, of course, Phi. Occult science has long since identified the Pentagram as the symbol of Man, the microcosm, the lesser universe, as opposed to the 6-pointed Star of David as that of the macrocosm, or greater universe. But what it has failed to recognize is that the Pentagram is actually the key to both worlds because of the Phi principle.

The Pentagram has also been the symbol for many secret societies, spanning the gap from modern-day Freemasonry and going all the way back to the days of Pythagoras. But again we reiterate: the secret of its power lies in the Golden Cut, and all the mathematics of Phi.

The Decagon

According to Pythagoras, the numerical symbol of the Macrocosmos or greater Universe was the Decad or the Ten. The nearest geometrical shape that corresponds to it is the Decagon, the 10-sided regular polygon that is formed by uniting 10 triangular increments of the Pentagram together at their apexes. Thus the Decagon, as well as the Pentagram, is a direct manifestation of the Phi principle.

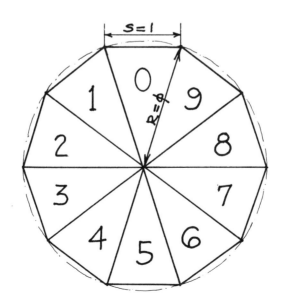

Here we find that the ratio of the *radius* of a circle in which a decagon is inscribed, to the length of one of its sides, is *exactly* $\frac{\phi}{1}$ or Phi, the Golden Mean, the Divine Proportion. Therefore, the Decagon is truly a universal key. We might call it the master key that unlocks all the doors to the Higher Consciousness, because it embraces each and every digit from the 0 to the 9.

Again, like the Pentagram, the secret of the power of the Decagon lies in the Golden number Phi. The ratio of its radius to one of its sides is always in a Phi proportion. Moreover, every lineal increment of its *internal* structure is also a Phi proportional to every other increment; that is, each rib is an individual term in the great Phi sequence of numbers.

The Golden Right Triangle

The proof that Phi is the one universal principle through which all things are brought into manifestation is derived from a reexamination of the Pythagorean theorem. This famous law states that the square of the hypotenuse of any right triangle is always equal to the sum of the squares of the other two sides. It is a universal law, applicable to *any* right triangle of *any* shape whatsoever, the only restriction being that two of the sides must be perpendicular to each other. The basic principle is expressed geometrically in the following diagram:

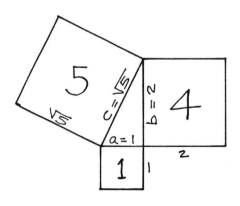

THE PYTHAGOREAN THEOREM

The square of the hypotenuse of any right triangle is always equal to the sum of the squares of the other two sides.

$$a^2 + b^2 = c^2$$

but

$$\frac{a^2}{b^2} \neq \frac{b^2}{c^2}$$

Therefore we find that the area of the 1st square, when added to the area of the 2nd square, is always equal to the area of the 3rd square. (The area of a square or the square of a number is the product of that number, multiplied by itself. Thus 4 is the square of 2, 9 the square of 3, etc.) Yet this particular aspect of the Pythagorean theorem is only part of the law, the other part being that the *ratios* between these lines or squares are *not* equal to each other. The only instance where they actually *are* equal is in the special case of the Golden Right Triangle, one triangle out of an infinite number of other right triangles with unequal ratios. A picture of this most beautiful of all right triangles follows below:

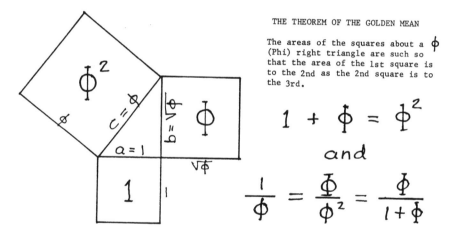

THE THEOREM OF THE GOLDEN MEAN

The areas of the squares about a ϕ (Phi) right triangle are such so that the area of the 1st square is to the 2nd as the 2nd square is to the 3rd.

$$1 + \phi = \phi^2$$

and

$$\frac{1}{\phi} = \frac{\phi}{\phi^2} = \frac{\phi}{1+\phi}$$

$$\phi = PHI = \frac{1+\sqrt{5}}{2} = 1.618034 = PROCeeD$$

Hence the areas of the squares about a Golden Right Triangle are such so that the area of the 1st square is to the area of the 2nd square, as the 2nd square is to the 3rd. Therefore, in this particular right triangle, not only does $a^2 + b^2 = c^2$, but the ratios between the sides are also equal, linearwise as well as areawise.

$$\frac{a}{b} = \frac{b}{c} \text{ and } \frac{a^2}{b^2} = \frac{b^2}{c^2}$$

The next step in our analysis is to determine mathematically the exact lengths of the sides of a Golden Right Triangle. If we make $a = 1$, it can be shown to our great delight and astonishment that b is then equal to the square root of Phi ($\sqrt{\phi}$), and c, the hypotenuse of the triangle, even equates to Phi (ϕ) itself!

This then, apparently, is the reason why the ancient Egyptians chose to use this particular triangle, the Golden Right Triangle of Phi (the *only* right triangle in which the sides are in equal proportion to each other), as the basis for the construction of that great monument to spirituality known as the Great Pyramid. For if you were to place an identical triangle back-to-back with the one in the figure, the combination of the two would give you an accurate cross section through the center of the Pyramid.

It follows then that Phi is the only number whose square root and 1 become the long and short sides, respectively, of a right triangle. Thus an infinite series of squares is born—with each successive square being the sum of the two preceding squares, as well as the next higher power of Phi.

$$1 + \phi = \phi^2$$
$$\phi + \phi^2 = \phi^3$$
$$\phi^2 + \phi^3 = \phi^4, \text{ etc.}$$

Is it any wonder then why the study of this particular triangle becomes all-important in the scheme of things?

The Pyramid/Tree of Life Glyph

It is a geometric law that the altitude of any right triangle drawn perpendicular to its hypotenuse divides the original triangle into two similar right triangles. This process can be repeated over and over again until we end up with a whole family of triangles. But in the special case of the Golden Right Triangle, not only are the areas of the triangles in a Phi sequence, but each line segment of both the altitude and the apothem (hypotenuse) are also in Phi proportion. Thus if we designate the triangles by the capital letters of the English alphabet, and the linear line segments by the lower-case letters, we can equate the triangles (B + C = D), or the altitude increments (y + a = c), or the apothem increments (z + b = d) in the following diagram of the Pyramid/Tree of Life.

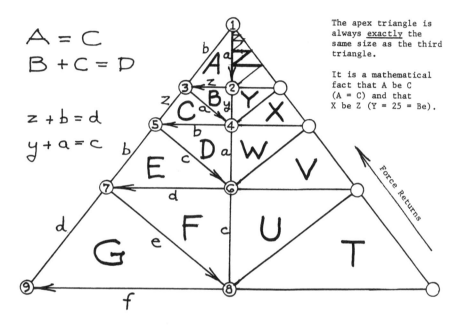

$A = C$

$B + C = D$

$z + b = d$

$y + a = c$

The apex triangle is always <u>exactly</u> the same size as the third triangle.

It is a mathematical fact that A be C (A = C) and that X be Z (Y = 25 = Be).

One can readily see that each term in the series (the areas or the line increments) is not only the sum of the two previous terms, but it also represents a consecutive power of the universal constant Phi (ϕ). See previous page.

The Apex of the Series and the Phi Mean

Now we come to a most important point, and a real key to the understanding of the true magic of Phi. It can easily be proved that in any Phi series of terms, *the value of the apex term is always exactly equal to the third term in the series.* We cannot overemphasize this point because it is a basic fundamental for any true understanding of this magical number. But where is the apex? The apex represents an infinite number of smaller terms, and it is always that which remains after we have stopped creating new terms in the series. At every point in the series there is always an apex, and the value of that apex is always numerically equal to the value of the term two steps away from where we are now. If you are at (C) in the following diagram, the apex is (A). The apex reflects (C). The Phi Mean, the B term in the series, is the doorway to the spiritual consciousness. The apex *is* the spiritual consciousness.

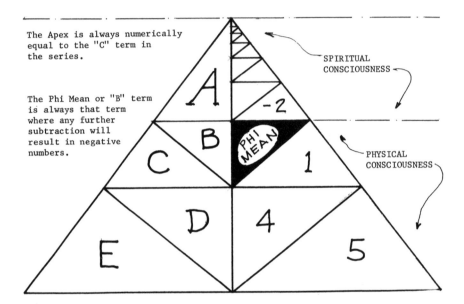

The Apex is always numerically equal to the "C" term in the series.

The Phi Mean or "B" term is always that term where any further subtraction will result in negative numbers.

SPIRITUAL CONSCIOUSNESS

PHYSICAL CONSCIOUSNESS

Thus we find that the Phi Mean acts as the doorway between the spiritual consciousness of the apex and the physical consciousness of the body of the pyramid, or between negative existence and positive existence. Now what do we mean by negative existence? Let us go back to the tabulation of Fibonacci numbers on page 76, where they were used to determine the number of rabbits at any point in time. This tabulation is what we might call *positive existence*, where each term is a positive number, being the sum of the two previous terms. This process is called successive addition.

But what would happen, let us say, if we were to reverse the process and compute the values of the terms in the upper part of the pyramid by successive subtraction? Eventually we would encounter negative numbers, and this state of consciousness, the spiritual state, is what is called *negative existence*.

The Phi Mean, then, is the doorway between these two states of consciousness—the spiritual state as opposed to the physical state, or negative existence as opposed to positive existence.

Examples Using the Phi Principle and the Pyramid/Tree of Life

Aside from the Fibonacci sequence of numbers, it is a mathematical fact that *any two numbers*, taken at random, when put through the process of successive addition and subtraction, will also bring Phi into manifestation. You can start with any two numbers you like, and when you add or subtract them successively, you are using the principle of Phi (successive addition is the same as multiplying by Phi, and successive subtraction is the same as dividing by Phi). Even after just a few computations, the ratios between the terms will be approximately equal to Phi (1.618034 to its nearest seven digits); the law being that the greater the number of terms, the closer will be the result.

It is best to start with successive subtraction, and continue the process until you reach zero (0), or until any further subtraction will result in a negative number. This represents the *Phi Mean* of the series, the doorway to the inner consciousness of the apex. In the Fibonacci sequence the Phi Mean actually *is* 0 (1 − 1 = 0); but in the average computation the Phi Mean will be the last number in the series before you reach a negative number. In any event, the Phi Mean is always a positive number or zero (0).

Then once the Phi Mean has been established (the B term in the series, just below the apex), the process can be continued indefinitely by successive addition, the object being to determine the numerical value of each and every term on the Pyramid/Tree of Life for the two particular words or numbers you are investigating. They may be *any* two words, and in *any* language, and through the magic of Phi you will be able to make a comprehensive analysis of their past, present, and future relationships. All you have to do is first ascertain the respective numbers of the words, and then after having placed them on the Tree of Life, allow the great power of the Phi law to reveal the story of what they have to tell.

Example 1

Let us now put the system to the test and see if it actually works. We could use any two words, but let us select two that are diametrically opposite to each other, such as the words NIGHT and DAY. Let us try to determine their relationships, what brought them into manifestation, and whither they are going. The steps in the process are outlined below:

Step 1: Determine the Alpha numbers of the words.
NIGHT = 58 = (14 + 9 + 7 + 8 + 20)
DAY   = 30 = (4 + 1 + 25)

Step 2: Put the two numbers through the process of successive subtraction, so that we can find where to place them on the Pyramid/Tree of Life. The value of their Phi Mean can usually be determined after only a few subtractions, and in this case it turns out to be 26: $(58 - 30 = 28)$, $(30 - 28 = 2)$, and $(28 - 2 = 26)$. Since $(2 - 26 = -24)$, a negative number, we know that the B term (the Phi Mean) of the Pyramid must be 26.

Step 3: The words can now be entered in their proper positions on the Pyramid/Tree of Life Glyph. The two key numbers are, of course, the Apex term and the Phi Mean; and after these numbers have been entered, the values of the remaining terms may be determined for all of the letters from A to Z by successive addition: i.e., each term is the sum of the two previous terms. The first seven terms from A to G have been included in the adjacent figure to show how the process works.

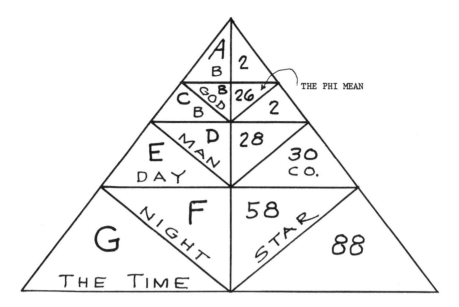

We are now ready to read the story of NIGHT and DAY, and see what they have to say. The word GOD may now be placed at the Phi Mean, since its Alpha number is 26. Likewise, we may place MAN in the *D* term because his number is 28. And the Apex, whose value is 2, just means "2 B" (to be). The rest of the story could be interpreted more or less along the following lines:

> Be God . . . Be Man.
> God is day. Man is night.
> God is to Man as day is to night.
> God is light. Man is darkness.

This certainly is an interesting conclusion! Or, perhaps we could say:

> Night and day, God be Man.
> Day and night, Man be God.
> Be God and Man, night and day.
> We are both Man and God!

Example 2

Another method of analysis is to play the Alpha number of a word against its Tarot number, and by so doing be able to climb to the apex of the Pyramid/Tree of Life when only one word is known. Let us use the word CHRIST and see what he can tell us about himself. The Alpha and Tarot values are computed as follows:

Alpha number of CHRIST = 77 = (3 + 8 + 18 + 9 + 19 + 20)

Tarot number of CHRIST = 75 = (18 + 9 + 16 + 1 + 17 + 14)

The second step will now be successive subtraction of the two terms, just like in the previous example: (77 − 75 = 2), (75 − 2 = 73), and (2 − 73 = −71). Thus we find that the *B* term of the Phi Mean is 73 (the last term in the series before we reach a negative number, which in this case is −71).

Now that we know the Phi Mean, we are ready to place the numbers in our Pyramid/Tree of Life glyph, just like before. Again the Apex turns out to be the number 2, and by successive addition of these two numbers (73 + 2), we can compute the value of each and every triangle in the Tree. The first seven terms are shown on the adjacent figure.

Since the Apex is always a repetition of the 3rd term in the series (the letter C), the English alphabet simply reaffirms the fact that A *Be* C (ABC), or that A equals C. And in this particular instance where the Apex is 2, it simply means "2 B" (to be). But CHRIST be what? (This is *his* Tree of Life, remember, because the values were computed on the basis of the Alpha and Tarot numbers of *his* name.) The Phi Mean gives us the answer. Its value is 73, the Alpha number for HERMIT, the key word for the 9th Tarot card whose symbol is the letter H, and whose *name* is ACHE or EACH.

Therefore, Christ becomes the Hermit (Tarot Key 9), the *Teacher* who holds his lantern aloft at the top of the mountain as he lights the way and beckons to *each* one of us to come unto Him and *be* as He.

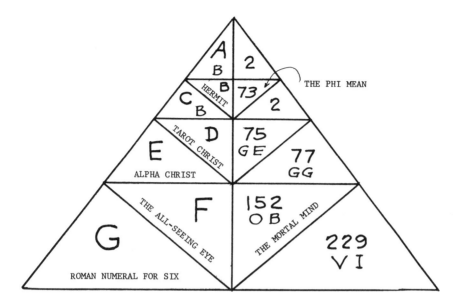

But this is only just a little of the story we can read from this glyph. Each and every triangle will have its own particular story to tell. For example, the F term is the number 152, which can be read O B (The Sun Be). The Sun is the center of the solar system, and it can be equated to Christ surrounded by his 12 disciples (the 12 signs of the Zodiac). But the number 152 is both positive and negative, inasmuch as it is the Alpha number for "The All-Seeing Eye" as well as "The Mortal Mind," the only "devil" that we will ever know if we are to believe the esoteric doctrine.

From these two examples we can readily see that if the words are properly named—which they must be, since the Cabalah teaches that it was the God Consciousness that named them in the first place—then the answers should all be there. If we dig deep enough, and far enough, into the Tree of Life, their past, present, and future relationships could very possibly become known. All it will take will be a good deal of concentrated effort on the part of the student. The rest is up to you.

NOTES

1. The Phi pattern in the human form is from an illustration in *The Curves of Life*, by Theodore Andrea Cook (New York, Dover Publications, Inc., 1979) page 467

2. The basic illustration of the facade of the Parthenon is from *The Parthenon and other Greek Temples: Their Dynamic Symmetry*, by Jay Hambidge (New Haven, Yale University Press, 1924) page XVII

3. The rabbit chart was adapted from an article by Verner E. Hoggatt, Jr. and illustrated by Bill Biderbost, titled "Number Theory: The Fibonacci Sequence," *1977 Yearbook of Science and the Future*, Encyclopaedia Britannica (The University of Chicago) pages 178–191

4. The pinecone figure was adapted from an illustration in *The Divine Proportion*, by H. E. Huntley (New York, Dover Publications, Inc., 1970) pages 161–165

5. Eliphas Levi, *Transcendental Magic* (New York, Samuel Weiser, 1974) page 239

6. The pentagram figure was adapted from a drawing in *Collectio Operum*, reprinted in *Man: The Grand Symbol of the Mysteries*, by Manly Palmer Hall (Los Angeles, The Philosophical Research Society, 1932, 1947) page 105

7. Other valuable reference books on Phi:

Matila Ghyka, *The Geometry of Art and Life* (New York, Dover Publications, 1977)

William Eisen, *The English Cabalah*, Vol. II, The Mysteries of Phi (Marina Del Rey, CA, DeVorss & Company, 1982)

William Eisen, *The Essence of the Cabalah* (Marina Del Rey, CA, DeVorss & Company, 1984)

CHAPTER FIVE

THE ENGLISH/HEBREW CABALAH:
ONE ENHANCING THE OTHER

t is evident that the ancient Hebrew mystics understood the Phi law. There are even further examples
that we will try to point out in this present chapter
showing their knowledge of these principles. Therefore in this part of the book we will combine the English Cabalah and the Hebrew Cabalah into one Cabalah, and thereby
achieve a new dimension in understanding.

But first we will attempt to weave into the pattern the five
basic elements that seem to constitute the foundation of Hebrew
mysticism. Or perhaps we should call them *concepts* since they
are not "elements" per se, but rather different viewpoints which
in the final analysis all lead to the ONENESS of the God Consciousness.

The first is the concept of AIN SOPH, the Infinite State,
that which has existed and always shall exist, and which is
beyond our present comprehension. The second is the LAW,
the Ten Commandments that were brought down by Moses
from Mt. Sinai, but more than that, they have a far deeper
and more significant meaning than is generally realized. If they
could be understood in their entirety, they would be seen as
only a single octave of a vast system of Cosmic Law.

The third concept is that of the Sephirothic Tree of Life. In

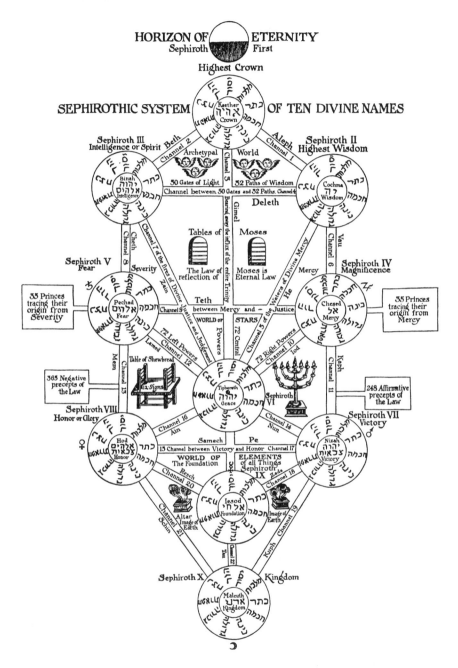

The Sephirothic Tree of Life Containing the Arcane Wisdom in Cabalistic Literature (After Kircher, "Oedipus Aegyptiacus," Rome, 1652) [1]

many ways the Ten Sephiroth are a *reflection* of the AIN SOPH, in much the same manner as the physical universe is a reflection of the spiritual universe. Therefore, God *is* AIN SOPH, but he manifests in the ten emanations of the Sephiroth. Thus all we perceive or know is set forth on the Sephirothic Tree; but Man, by dedicating himself to this wisdom, has the power to raise himself back up to his heavenly state.

The fourth and fifth concepts are really subdivisions of the third. In the fourth, the Sephirothic Tree is *divided* into its three basic Pillars, the Pillars of the Temple, as it were; while in the fifth concept it is *multiplied* into the four Worlds. Yet in all five of these concepts we will endeavor to use the English Cabalah to enhance them and make them more comprehensive. And it has the power to do this quite well, since the language of symbology is the language of the soul.

AIN SOPH (the Infinite State)

In the beginning, before the very dawn of time, was AIN SOPH. It represents that which remains after every knowable thing has been removed—the incomprehensible state of pure *Being*. It is circular in shape, being depicted as a giant globe outside of which there is nothing, not even a vacuum (see adjacent figure). Therefore, AIN SOPH bears the same relationship to the created Universe as the Auric Egg bears to the body of Man. It is the great Cosmic Egg, within which the creation and dissolution of absolutely everything of any nature whatsoever is constantly taking place. AIN SOPH is therefore the Absolute, all there is, the infinite as opposed to the finite, within which the Core of Life is only a mere dot.

Yet the nature of AIN SOPH is itself divided into three parts: (1) AIN, Nothing or Negative Existence, the vacuum of Pure Spirit; (2) AIN SOPH, the Limitless and Boundless; and (3) AIN SOPH AUR, the Limitless Light. These may be depicted as circular rings within the area of a circle; but in the beginning the Supreme Substance, the AIN, alone permeated the entire area of the circle. Then, as this Substance moved in towards the center of itself, the ring of AIN SOPH was brought into manifestation, which in reality was a limitation of AIN; and finally the third ring of AIN SOPH AUR, or Light, came into Being, which represented a still further limitation. These then all surround that which remains—the physical body of the Universe (the macrocosm), or the physical body of Man himself (the microcosm).

The Auric Egg of the Soul

We find that the Universal Consciousness of God or the Individual Consciousness of Man is in this aura, which extends in all directions and completely encircles its lower bodies. The AIN SOPH is therefore that from which all emanations come forth. It is the primal world in which the soul of man is in perfect harmony with God.

But the AIN itself, or Negative Existence, is what might be referred to as infinite energy. It is not in the created world but in its own state of consciousness. It is the beginning and the end of the created world. As Carl Jung has indicated in his work, "It (the Supreme Substance) penetrates the created world as the sunlight penetrates the air everywhere. Although it penetrates it completely, the created world has no part of it, just as an utterly transparent body does not become either dark or light in color as the result of the passage of light through it."

Many times in the Hebrew Cabalah the additive principles of the Phi law are demonstrated, but this fact has strangely gone unnoticed by today's cabalistic community. As to why this situation should exist is anybody's guess, but it is clearly evident that the *ancient* Hebrew scholars were well aware of these principles. For example: let us study the numerical values of the three words contained in the "Limitless Light" of AIN SOPH AUR. The Hebrew spellings of the words along with their numerical values are as follows:

Hebrew Words	*Hebrew Letters*		*Total Values*
A I N	Aleph (1) + Yod (10) + Nun (50)	= 61	First
+ S V P	Samekh (60) + Vav (6) + Pe (80)	= 146	+ Second
= A V R	Aleph (1) + Vav (6) + Resh (200)	= 207	= Third

Here we find that the spellings of these words were set up in such a manner so that the numerical value of the first term, when added to that of the second, brings the third term into manifestation. These, of course, are the basic principles of the Phi law.

Now let us do the same computations with the equivalent words in English. Sometimes by comparing the Hebrew Cabalah with the English Cabalah, valuable additional information can be forthcoming. The results follow below:

English Words and Alpha Numbers		English Translation		Hebrew Words and Numerical Values	
AIN	= 24	Nothingness = 144		A I N	= 61
SOPH	= 58	Limitless	= 118	S V P	= 146
Sum	= 82	Sum	= 262	Sum	= 207
AUR	= 40	Light	= 56	A V R	= 207
Difference	= 42	Difference	= 206	Difference =	0
	(The I)		B OF = B		

And again we have confirmation of the amazing interplay between the English and Hebrew systems. The difference between the Alpha value of the English "AUR" and what its Phi value should be is 42, the Alpha number of "The I." And the difference between the Alpha value of "Light" and its theoretical Phi value is 206, the Alpha number of "The Wheel of Fortune," the name of Tarot Key 10 whose symbol is the letter B. Thus the message that "The I B" seems to be similar to the "BE I" we received when analyzing the names of the Tarot cards making up the word GOD (see Chapter 3, page 57). And the combination of all three differences spells out BIO, meaning Life.

When we used these Phi principles of consecutive addition and subtraction in the two examples at the end of Chapter 4, we calculated the Phi Mean term of the Pyramid/Tree of Life, but we did not continue any further up into its spiritual apex. The Phi Mean, you will remember, was either zero (0) or the last positive number before reaching a negative number during the process of consecutive subtraction.

But what would have happened had we continued the process indefinitely, subtracting each term, the one from the other, and thereby projecting ourselves up *into* the spiritual apex of the pyramid? Would the numbers be getting smaller and smaller and smaller? Surprisingly they would not. Instead, once the Phi Mean term was reached, the numbers would start *increasing* again in magnitude, the only difference being that the *sign* of each term would alternate between positive and negative values.

It follows then that the *apex* of a Pyramid/Tree of Life (the spiritual consciousness as opposed to the physical consciousness) is not a relatively small term at the top of the pyramid at all; but rather it becomes a large, *inverted* pyramid equally as great as the body of the physical pyramid upon which it rests.

Therefore, a new diagram is in order that will more correctly portray the Pyramid/Tree of Life as it *really* is, and not in the way we normally view it with the entire spiritual universe folded and compressed into the unrealistic state depicted in the illustrations in the previous chapter. So then let us now expand our consciousness, unfold the soul so to speak, and by so doing also unfold our Pyramid/Tree of Life to the point where it can be viewed in its entirety. The act is accomplished by simply transferring our attention to the figure on the following page.

We have designated the values of the terms by the Fibonacci sequence of numbers, but in a practical analysis any sequence would work just as well. But the Fibonacci sequence is unique in that the Phi Mean actually *is* 0, and the values of the terms in the spiritual consciousness are equal and opposite to their counterparts in the physical consciousness in the body of the lower pyramid.

We have also identified the terms in the right-hand half of the pyramid as those pertaining to AIN SOPH, as opposed to those in the left-hand side which represent AIN SOPH AUR. But the entire apex, it should be noted, is permeated by the infinite energy of the AIN itself, the Supreme Substance that

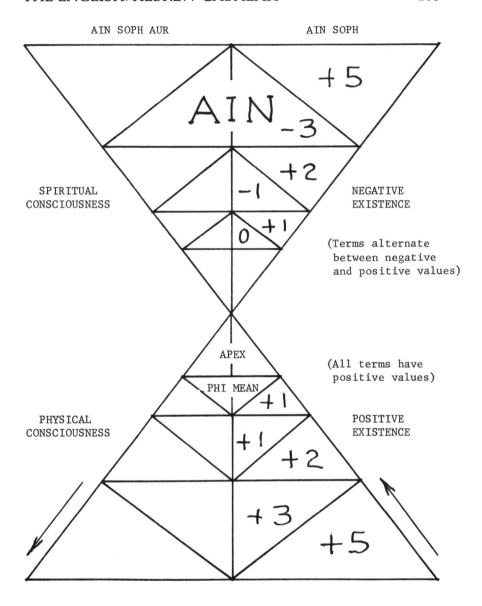

The True Relationship between the Physical and Spiritual Aspects of a Pyramid/Tree of Life

enables the positive and negative aspects of its other two facets to exist.

The AIN is therefore true Negative Existence (or Nothing, as it is sometimes called), because when the positive and negative terms which comprise the *total* Consciousness of AIN SOPH and AIN SOPH AUR are added together, the negative values will almost, but not quite, annihilate the positive values, with the net result that the total magnitude of the AIN is close to zero (Nothing).

The reader will profit by spending as much time as he needs in studying the preceding figure in order to understand completely the principles involved. Although the diagram may appear strange on the surface, it is only because we are not accustomed to viewing the spiritual "negatively existent" universe and the physical universe at one and the same time.

We may expand our two pyramids upward and downward for as many terms as we wish, and by so doing, embrace more and more of the infinite universe as term after term is unveiled before our eyes. Yet we can still never reach the ultimate, as there will always be still other terms beyond the scope of our consciousness, no matter how high we had gone. Yet this is not entirely true because we can always replace the golden apex once more upon the inverted pyramid (the next-to-the-highest term that we were able to reach), thus keeping the mathematics of the Phi sequence in the same valid condition that it was in originally. Every term in the pyramid—in the upper spiritual pyramid or in the lower physical pyramid— is still the sum total of everything that had gone on before, with the sole exception of the one immediately preceding it.

Another aspect of the two pyramids, the one above the other, is that they resemble an hourglass. And the symbol of the hourglass illustrates one of the most basic and fundamental principles of Cabalah in that it points out the constant interplay between the forces of birth, life, death, and their inevitable resurrection and rebirth. These then go on to form a continuous chain of events that governs everything in the universe, even the very principle of time itself.

For example: Time is "born" the moment you turn the hour-glass upside down, thus putting the process in operation. And when the last particles of sand have fallen from the upper chamber into the lower chamber, the process stops and death is the result. Thus we could say that Time "lived" all during the time the particles were falling and in motion, but at the moment this activity ceased, all was still and Time "died." And Time continued to remain "dead," perhaps even for several years of our time, until you brought it back to life again when you started the process in operation once more.

Who did we say brought it back to life again? It was *You.* *You* were the one who started the process operating, but it was the universal laws of *God* that kept the particles moving in their journey from the upper chamber into the lower chamber. Thus all that Man can do is initiate a process; it is God that doeth the work. Here again is another fundamental principle of Cabalah. That principle is that Man is a co-partner with God. One cannot manifest without the other, in the sense that for every image there must also exist that which makes the image. The reflection cannot exist without the reality.

The Ten Commandments

Moses Maimonides, the great Jewish philosopher of the twelfth century, in describing the Tables of the Law written by the finger of God, divides all productions into two general orders: products of Nature and products of art. God works through Nature and man through art, he asserts in his *Guide for the Perplexed.* Thus the Word of the Lord is the hand, or active principle, by which the will of the Creator is traced upon the face of His creation.[2]

Moreover, we have from no less an authority than Manly Palmer Hall that the Tannaim, the initiates of the Jewish Mystery School, alone possessed a complete understanding of the significance of the Ten Commandments. These laws are esoterically related to the Ten Sephiroth and the Pillars upon which they are placed to make the Tree of Life. Thus through these ten degrees of contemplation along the Path of Ecstasy, the

Moses Receiving the Tables of the Law
—From an Old Bible

initiate could thereby follow this Path that winds upward through the four worlds, and eventually ends in the magnificence of AIN SOPH.

It would be very good at this point to go back in time and try to see the analogy of where we are coming from and where we are going. In other words, we want to understand the background for these symbols, the background being the *Ten Commandments* brought to us by Moses from Mt. Sinai.

Manly Palmer Hall, in *The Secret Teachings of All Ages*, gives us our first clue. He quotes Hargrave Jennings as saying: "The Ten Commandments are inscribed in two groups of five each, in columnar form. The five to the right (looking from the altar) mean the 'Law'; the five to the left mean the 'Prophets.' The right stone is masculine, the left stone is feminine. They correspond to the two disjoined pillars of stone (or towers) in the front of every cathedral, and of every temple in the heathen times." The same author states that the Law is masculine because it was delivered direct from the Deity, while the Prophets, or Gospels, were feminine because they were born through the nature of man.[3]

But Mr. Hall himself goes on to say: "The right Tablet of the Law further signifies *Jachin*—the white pillar of light; the left Tablet, *Boaz*—the shadowy pillar of darkness. These were the names of the two pillars cast from brass set up on the porch of King Solomon's Temple. . . . These two pillars respectively connote also the active and the passive expressions of Divine Energy, the sun and the moon, sulphur and salt, good and bad, light and darkness.

"In the mysterious Sephirothic Tree of the Jews, these two pillars symbolize Mercy and Severity. Standing before the gate of King Solomon's Temple, these columns had the same symbolic import as the obelisks before the sanctuaries of Egypt. . . . On one side towered the stupendous column of the intellect; on the other, the brazen pillar of the flesh. Midway between these two stands the glorified wise man, but he cannot reach this high estate without first suffering upon the cross made by joining these pillars together. The early Jews occa-

THE HIGH PRIESTESS

sionally represented the two pillars, Jachin and Boaz, as the legs of Jehovah, thereby signifying to the modern philosopher that Wisdom and Love, in their most exalted sense, support the whole order of creation—both mundane and supermundane."[3]

We find that the Ten Commandments can be directly related to the pillars of King Solomon's Temple, as well as the pillars of the Sephirothic Tree. Ten is the number of perfection, the proper symbol of God, Man, and the Universe. It is the sacred Ten which Jehovah has given to us as the key for understanding the Cosmic Scheme that controls all things.

Now let us use English Cabalah to enhance our understanding of "The Ten Commandments" using the Alpha numbers of the words.

THE TEN COMMANDMENTS = (33 + 39 + 134)   = 206
THE WHEEL OF FORTUNE   = (33 + 53 + 21 + 99) = 206

In the design of Tarot Key 10, The Wheel of Fortune, are the letters TAROT which mean "Wheel of the *Law*." Also on the Wheel of Fortune card are the letters I H V H which spell the word *God* in Hebrew. Therefore, we can conclude *The Ten*

Commandments, when interpreted in the light of the Cabalah, literally are *God's Law*.

We also find that the *Alpha* symbol for the Wheel of Fortune is the letter *B*, while its *Tarot* number is *10*, which equates to the letter *J*. Here we have a very good confirmation that the two tablets on which Moses gave us the Ten Commandments are represented by the pillars Boaz and Jachin on either side of the entrance to King Solomon's Temple:

$$2 = B = Boaz \qquad 10 = J = Jachin$$

This refers us directly to the High Priestess (Tarot Key 2), who is shown seated between the black Pillar of Boaz (B) and the white Pillar of Jachin (J). She then acts as the Middle Pillar, the intermediary between the two Outer Pillars. Furthermore, the Alpha number of her name (195), when reduced to the next smaller number (19 + 5), equates to 24, the English letter X, and the Roman numeral for 10.

The Sephirothic Tree of Life

The Sephirothic Tree of Life is the primary symbol of Cabalah. The philosophy is one of evolution. Out of the "nothingness" our cosmos developed through 32 paths of wisdom. The first ten paths are the manifestation of the Sephiroth themselves, beginning with the pure spirit of Kether the Crown, and ending with the material or physical Kingdom of Malkuth. Once this base point of the 10th Sephirah was reached, the universe began an upwards process of reabsorption along the 22 interconnecting paths between the Sephiroth.

Therefore the Tree of Life is a picture of Creation. Cast in the form of an analogic tree, it demonstrates the flow of forces down from the Divine to the lowest world and back again. The Universe hovers between these two poles, which may be described mathematically as All or Nothing. Either end of the axis may be seen as the Nothing, or then again it might become the All, the exact condition depending upon whether it is serving as an entry or exit point.

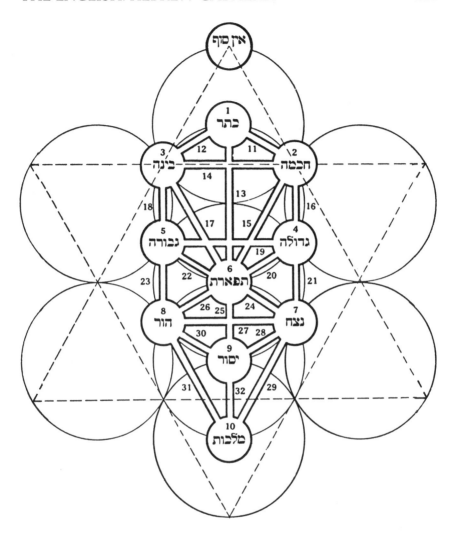

The Star of David or the Seal of Solomon Becomes Plainly Evident in this Diagram of the AIN SOPH and the TEN SEPHIROTH Showing the 32 Paths of Wisdom and the Geometry of the Tree of Life[4]

The *Sepher Sephiroth* (Book of Emanations) describes the gradual evolution of the Deity from negative Paradise or Heaven, into positive existence. (Positive existence is the physical universe.) Yet the AIN SOPH and the Sephiroth are inseparable. AIN SOPH is God, and He manifests himself in ten emanations which are called the ten Sephiroth. The emanation from AIN SOPH thus permeates the Sephiroth with its light and luminescence, the light flowing through the Sephiroth which they need for their existence.

The Sephiroth act as spheres or vessels through which the *light of God is emanated unto man.* The singular form of the word is *Sephirah,* as opposed to its plural form which is *Sephiroth.* It may be loosely translated as a numerical emanation or intelligence. In Cabalah, the two words (the singular or the plural) refer to ten creative world powers in which the original Divine Being is manifested in separate stages.

In the beginning the AIN SOPH (the uppermost sphere in the diagram) merges with the Crown of Kether, the 1st Sephirah at the top of the Tree of Life. It then proceeds through the ten numbers (the ten Sephiroth) on down to the Kingdom of Malkuth at the base of the Tree. The 22 interconnecting paths are usually associated with the 22 letters of the Hebrew alphabet.

Yet in the beginning even the lowest kingdom (Malkuth) represented the consciousness of men raised to the spiritual level. The ten Sephiroth, each of which acts as the outer shell of the next, were also associated, as we said earlier, with the ten original words (corresponding with the Ten Commandments).

In summary: The Tree of the Sephiroth, which is sometimes called the Tree of Life, represents different states of consciousness by the Sephiroth as they are numbered one through ten. The 22 paths between the Sephiroth stand for subjective experiences (arising from conditions within, and not caused by external stimuli) which the individual psyche undergoes while its consciousness travels to the next path.

The Sephiroth are linked to one another by "canals" or "roads" along which it is possible for the consciousness of the soul to ascend or descend as the case might be. Each Sephirah then acts as a place or a station where we may stay for awhile, as opposed to the paths which become roads for continuous movement. You might say that the Sephiroth are used as stations for climbing the Tree of Life in order to regain heaven.

In the symbology of the Tarot, the ten Sephiroth may be identified by the numbered cards of the Minor Arcana from the Ace to the Ten. But in that case, the 22 paths would be represented by the 22 cards of the Major Arcana.

The Sephirothic Doctrine is referred to in many cabalistic sources, including the *Sepher Yetzirah*, and with a large number of variants in the *Bahir*, and in the *Zohar*. For example:

"The Ten ineffable Sephiroth have ten vast regions bound unto them; boundless in origin and having no ending; an abyss of good and of ill; measureless height and depth; boundless to the East and the West; boundless to the North and South; and the Lord the only God, the Faithful King rules all these from his holy seat, for ever and ever." (*Sepher Yetzirah* I:5)[5]

The commonly accepted English spelling for the Hebrew names of the Sephiroth, along with their English translations, are shown in the following figure. This particular diagram of the Tree of Life is the way most Cabalists view it today. Therefore, a brief description of the attributes of the ten Sephiroth would now be helpful, so that the student could at least have a general idea of their individual meanings. We will cover them in the order of their manifestation, from the one to the ten.

1. KETHER (*Crown*): This 1st Sephirah at the tip of the tree is called the great "I AM," and it represents the supreme individualization of the Universal Essence. Being unity, it is incapable of multiplication by itself, since $1 \times 1 \times 1 \times 1 \ldots$ etc. is always equal to 1. How then, can the number 2 be brought into manifestation? The answer is by the *reflection* of the number 1, which is often referred to as the Monad.

2. CHOKMAH (*Wisdom*): The 2nd Sephirah at the top of the right-hand pillar is the Duad, which is composed of the reality, the number 1, *and* its reflection. Ultimate benevolence, expressed as true wisdom, is its chief characteristic.

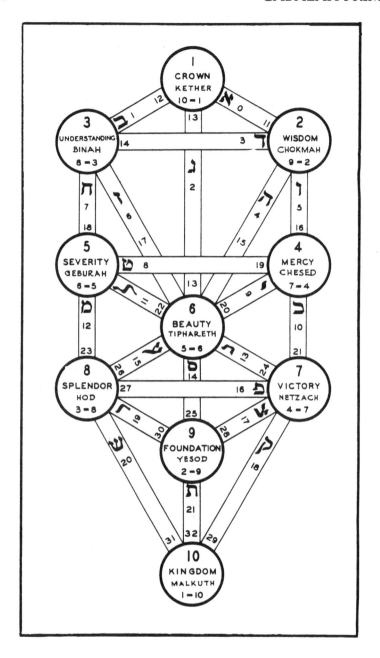

The Modern Version of the Sephirothic Tree of Life
Along with Its 32 Paths of Wisdom[6]

3. BINAH (*Understanding*): The 3rd Sephirah balances the 2nd Sephirah, and heads the pillar at the left-hand side of the tree. It represents the Triad, and everything that is associated with the number 3. Binah is the Supernal Mother, and the giver of life. Many have referred to her as the Holy Ghost, the 3rd member of the Trinity.

4. CHESED (*Mercy*): The 4th Sephirah is also called *Gedulah*, which means love. Greatness and magnificence are some of its attributes, and anything that pertains to comfort, rest, and refreshment. Chesed is the great comforter.

5. GEBURAH (*Severity*): This Sephirah is stern and powerful, and it represents Justice. It is the opposite force of Chesed (Mercy) and thus balances it. You might say it represents the retributive aspects of *karma* (the law of cause and effect).

6. TIPHARETH (*Beauty*): The 6th Sephirah is at the exact center of the Tree, and indeed it is the most "beautiful" of all the stations the soul visits in its journey from the physical to the spiritual. It corresponds to the solar plexus of the human anatomy, and it is the abode of the soul. Therefore, it represents the Christ force.

7. NETZACH (*Victory*): The basic characteristic of this Sephirah is great feeling, or emotion. There is also a good deal of sentiment attached to this particular way station, insofar as it represents the first sense of feeling victorious after having conquered and freed oneself from the restrictions of the physical.

8. HOD (*Splendor*): The 8th Sephirah is often called Glory. Its basic characteristic is that it represents the power of the mind, the *mental* aspect of Being. But the mind is often the slayer of the real; therefore, its aspects are both positive and negative.

9. YESOD (*Foundation*): The 9th Sephirah is in the middle pillar directly above the 10th Sephirah of Malkuth. If the reader would picture the entire Tree as the body of Man seated in meditation with his legs crossed beneath him, his feet would

be in Malkuth, his head would be in Kether, and his *sexual* function, or the seat of the kundalini force (the base of the spine), would be at *Yesod.* Therefore, the basic attribute of this Sephirah is that it is the seat of psychological forces, and all that they imply.

10. MALKUTH (*Kingdom*): This 10th Sephirah at the base of the Tree represents the physical world and where we are at right now. But it is also the point where the physical and spiritual forces touch each other, and is therefore the doorway to the higher realms. Inasmuch as its number is 10, it has a direct affinity with the crown Sephirah of Kether, whose number is 1. We will say more about this a little later in the chapter.

The Three Pillars

The 6th verse of the first chapter of the *Sepher Yetzirah* reads as follows: "The Ten ineffable Sephiroth have the appearance of *the Lightning flash,* their origin is unseen and no end is perceived. The Word is in them as they rush forth and as they return, they speak as from the whirlwind, and returning fall prostrate in adoration before the Throne."[5]

The key words here are the "lightning flash," and if anyone has ever watched the zig-zag path of a lightning bolt as it grounds itself into the earth, he would have to agree that it looks very much like the illustration in the adjoining figure. This, then, is what eventually gave rise to the three pillars of the Sephirothic Tree as it is known today.

The left-hand pillar is called the Pillar of Severity, and it corresponds to the black pillar of Boaz in the Masonic tradition. The right-hand pillar is called the Pillar of Mercy, and it corresponds to the white pillar of Jachin. Both of these pillars occupy prominent positions on either side of the entrance to Solomon's Temple. This leaves then the middle pillar, the position occupied by the High Priestess in Tarot Key 2, and it is called the Pillar of Mildness.

It is as Eliphas Levi has written: "In Kabbalah, these Pillars explain all mysteries of antagonism, whether natural, political, or religious. They elucidate also the procreative struggle be-

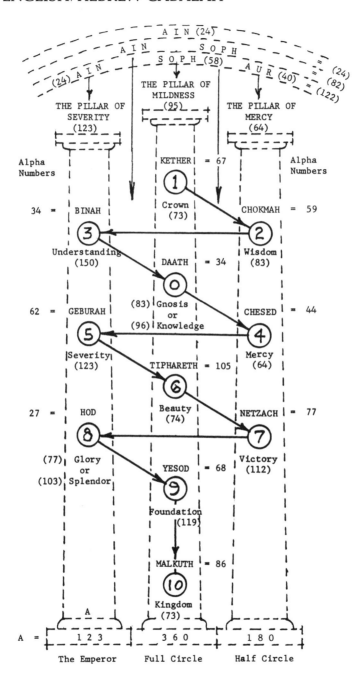

The Three Pillars of the Sephirothic Tree

tween man and woman." Opposites are therefore present in the Pillars of Jachin and Boaz. They are to each other as male and female, the positive and the negative, light and darkness, etc. The *Zohar* refers to the Middle Pillar as the perfect pillar, and with the three pillars combined, the Sephiroth are able to enter into a new relationship with one another. The two outer Pillars of Mercy and Severity are balanced by the middle Pillar of Mildness.

Before we get into a cabalistic analysis of the names of the Sephiroth on each of the pillars, a further explanation is necessary. You will note that the empty space on the Middle Pillar between Kether and Tiphareth is occupied by another Sephirah, which is called *Daath*. In English, the word means Gnosis or Knowledge. This Sephirah is not a true Sephirah in the sense of the word, but rather it means the *absence* of a Sephirah, the vacant space formerly occupied by Malkuth (the 10th Sephirah at the base of the tree) before its fall into the earthly realms of matter. Daath, therefore, represents the Abyss, the Pit, or whatever other terminology you wish to give it. It represents the digit 0 (Nothing), as opposed to the number 10 (the All).

Now let us see how the *English* spelling of these *Hebrew* words enhances their original cabalistic meanings. Let us begin with the left-hand Pillar of Severity. The Alpha numbers for the *Hebrew* names of the Sephiroth on this pillar are as follows:

BINAH	= (2 + 9 + 14 + 1 + 8)	=	34
GEBURAH	= (7 + 5 + 2 + 21 + 18 + 1 + 8)	=	62
HOD	= (8 + 15 + 4)	=	27
	Total Value	=	123

But this number is not only the same as the Alpha number for the *English* name of the entire pillar, but it also brings the Emperor himself into manifestation:

SEVERITY = 123 = THE EMPEROR = 123 (Tarot Key 4), the letter A

Now let us look at the other two pillars. The Alpha numbers follow below:

The Pillar of Mildness				The Pillar of Mercy		
KETHER	=	67		CHOKMAH	=	59
DAATH	=	34				
TIPHARETH	=	105		CHESED	=	44
YESOD	=	68				
MALKUTH	=	86		NETZACH	=	77
Total	=	360° (full circle)		Total	=	180° (half circle)

But we are not through yet. The Alpha number for MILD-NESS is 95, the same as EMPRESS (95), the counterpart of the Emperor. Furthermore, it is also the same as "I AM THAT I AM" ($9 + 14 + 49 + 9 + 14 = 95$), the perfect name for the Middle Pillar. Now we can see how the English enhances and amplifies these Hebrew words.

The Four Worlds

Now that we understand the general nature of the ten Sephiroth, we will explore the greater design of the Cabalists which consists of not one, but *four* different worlds of creation. Thus the light from the original ten Sephiroth, through the process of reflection, gradually poured into four great world chains, four symbolical trees known as (1) *Atziluth*, the Boundless World of Emanations; (2) *Briah*, the Archangelic World of Creations; (3) *Yetzirah*, the Hierarchal World of Formations; and (4) *Assiah*, the Physical World of Substances, or the World of Action.

These four realms form a chain of increasing density. Each world is a fainter reflection of the one above it, while at the same time becoming denser and denser. And when we reach Assiah (the world in which we live), the environment is so dense that we can't see far beyond ourselves. But *it is the nature of these worlds to interpenetrate each other*, in much the same way as radio or TV frequencies move through physical matter. Therefore these higher worlds exist simultaneously, vibrating at different rates of frequency all around us.

Yet we should mention frequencies even lower than those of the physical. These are the *Qliphoth*, the evil and adverse Sephiroth, and they exist in the Elemental World deep within the earth itself. Yet the Qliphoth are not independent of the Sephiroth of the Physical World, but rather they represent the unbalanced and destructive aspects of the Holy Stations (Sephiroth) themselves. A Qliphah could then be seen as the reverse of a coin of which the obverse is a Sephirah. They are sometimes called shells, and they are better known as *hell*. Man creates this shell-like Qliphah with his mortal mind and negative thinking. His mortal mind then becomes his own hell.[7]

A diagram of these four Sephirothic Trees or world chains appears on the following page. Yet we must remember that the overall consciousness of the entity called Man contains not just one of these Sephirothic Trees, but a combination of all of them. In Man, they correspond to different levels of his Being. The physical (Assiah) is the lowest realm. This is then followed by the mental (Yetzirah), the emotional (Briah), and the spiritual (Atziluth), which is the topmost tree of them all.

Therefore, while Man lives in the Assiatic World, he has access to the upper Universes when he finally evolves and refines his being. But while he is still on the earth plane, God assists him through his chakras, the elements, the planets, and the Zodiac.

In Yetzirah, God acts through the Hierarchy, through Angelic Orders such as the Ten Angelic Hosts, etc. In Briah, he acts through the mediation of the Archangels. But in Atziluth, the highest world of them all, God deals directly, and not through his ministers. That is why it is called the World of Emanations, the emanations of the *Divine Names*, whereby God—which is a consciousness, mind you, and not an individual—exists through and by the powers of his Name.

We previously learned that Paths 1 through 10 brought the Sephiroth themselves into manifestation, and that Paths 11

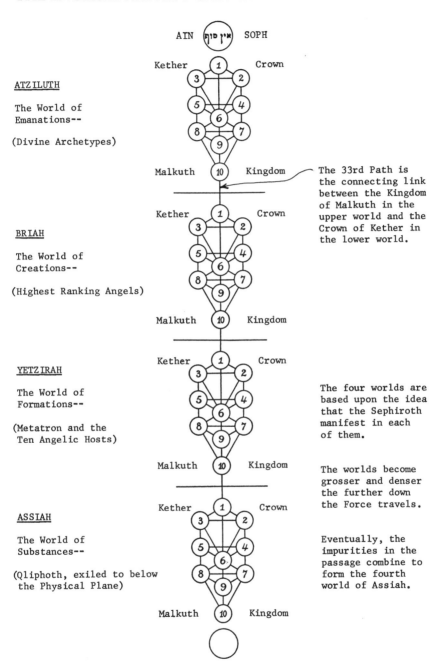

AIN (אין סוף) SOPH

Kether ① Crown

ATZILUTH

The World of
Emanations--

(Divine Archetypes)

Malkuth ⑩ Kingdom

The 33rd Path is
the connecting link
between the Kingdom
of Malkuth in the
upper world and the
Crown of Kether in
the lower world.

Kether ① Crown

BRIAH

The World of
Creations--

(Highest Ranking Angels)

Malkuth ⑩ Kingdom

Kether ① Crown

YETZIRAH

The World of
Formations--

(Metatron and the
Ten Angelic Hosts)

The four worlds are
based upon the idea
that the Sephiroth
manifest in each
of them.

Malkuth ⑩ Kingdom

The worlds become
grosser and denser
the further down
the Force travels.

Kether ① Crown

ASSIAH

The World of
Substances--

(Qliphoth, exiled to below
the Physical Plane)

Eventually, the
impurities in the
passage combine to
form the fourth
world of Assiah.

Malkuth ⑩ Kingdom

The Four Sephirothic Trees[8]

through 32 were the 22 roads or pathways that connected them. But what, then, should we call the 33rd Path, the one that connects the four worlds into a continuous chain?

The answer is that it is much the same as the 33rd degree in Freemasonry. This Path is bestowed but never trod. It represents a quantum jump from one state of consciousness to another. Therefore, it is not the same as the other Paths because of the ancient cabalistic axiom which states, "Kether is in Malkuth." Thus Kether, the Crown of the lower Tree, exists *within* Malkuth, the Kingdom of the Tree immediately above it. They are one and the same because there is no first and last Sephirah in the ordinary sense. If Kether seems remote from Malkuth, it is not because it is far away in time and space, but rather because the consciousness in Malkuth is not aware of Kether's presence. Thus the Cabalah affirms the immediate possibility of self-realization, if and when the disciple on the Path removes the final veil and finds that they are ONE.

Now is there any further proof that what we say here is true? Yes there is, and it lies within the English Cabalah. The English translation for Kether (the 1st Sephirah) is *Crown;* and the English translation for Malkuth (the 10th Sephirah) is *Kingdom.* The Alpha numbers of the terms follow below:

Number	Name	Alpha Number
1	CROWN (Kether)	73
10	KINGDOM (Malkuth)	73
1 + 10	ONE (34) + TEN (39)	73

Thus: (ONE + TEN) = CROWN = KINGDOM = 73

By comparing the Alpha numbers of the terms, we find that they are identical. Heaven is in the earth, and the earth is in heaven. Or, perhaps we should say that the earth is the *outer shell* of heaven. Why? Because if Kether (the crown of the lower tree) is in Malkuth (the kingdom of the upper tree), then Malkuth must enclose it and act as its outer shell.

The *Zohar* (Book of Splendor) further explains this principle by stating: "Upper and lower, from the first mystic point up to the furthest removed of all the stages, are all coverings to one another." Therefore, this most fundamental principle of cabalistic lore stresses over and over again that all creatures are interwoven. The major teachers of this body of knowledge have repeatedly stated that each aspect of creation, even including the Cosmos itself, is connected to everything else. The most central thought of this study is the ever-recurring message: "As above, so below." What we think, what we say, the way we act—each has an influence on the whole.

Cabalists stress that as we reach higher states of awareness, we will begin to see more of the unity among the apparent opposites. For example: Chapter I, Verse 7, of the *Sepher Yetzirah* reads as follows: "The Ten ineffable Sephiroth, whose ending is even as their origin, are like as a flame arising from a burning coal. For God is superlative in his Unity, there is none equal unto Him: what number canst thou place before One?"[5]

Now let us move on to still other methods of observing this fourfold classification of all things. And even in the Cabalah, it has far-reaching significance. First and foremost there are the four worlds. These are followed by the four elements: earth, water, air, and fire, which is only another way of describing the four states of matter: its solid, liquid, gaseous, and energy states, respectively. These also appear again in the four basic divisions of the signs of the Zodiac.

Then there are the four suits of the Tarot Minor Arcana: Pentacles, Cups, Swords, and Wands. These are followed by the four Living Creatures of Ezekiel's vision, which again are symbols of the four worlds. First there is the Heavenly Man, the Adam Kadmon of Masonic tradition, representing the Divine Domain of Emanations. Then there is the eagle, symbolizing the World of Cosmic Creation; and he is followed in turn by the lion, representing the World of Formation; and the bull, the earthly level of the World of Action.

Even the science of the 20th century gets into the act, by proclaiming that there are only *four* basic forces in the universe: the *weak* force, the *strong* force, the *electromagnetic* force, and the *gravitational* force. And then there is the law of the four colors used in mapping, which states that you need *four* colors, and four colors only, to color in the various divisions of a map so that no country, no matter how large or small you make them, will touch another country with the same color.

The members of the Pythagorean Brotherhood (580–500 B.C.) bound themselves not to betray their mathematical and other secrets by an oath taken in the name of the *Tetractys*. These ten dots, or commas, were a symbol of the greatest importance, for it revealed that the sum of the first *four* integers equates to ten $(1 + 2 + 3 + 4 = 10)$.

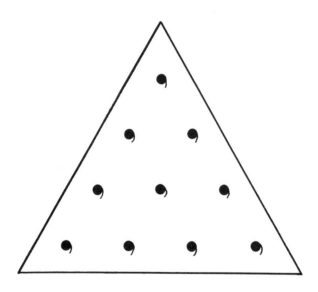

The Tetractys of the Pythagoreans[9]

Hence we find, through the symbol of this ancient Brotherhood, the real secret of the Decad or the Ten. We can start to count, but it takes the sum of the first *four* numbers before we return once more to the One (10 is the first number that reduces to 1).

The Ten Tetractys can also be equated to the Ten Commandments, or to the Ten Sephiroth of the Tree of Life. But these are not the only examples in the Cabalah where the universal mystery of this aspect of the Decad is brought to our attention. Not by any means. The following tabulation of the Alpha numbers of the names of the ten Tarot cards whose symbols are the letters A through J (the first 10 letters of the English alphabet) will emphasize it even further:

Alpha No. of Card	Symbol of Card	Name of Tarot Card	Alpha No. of Name
1	A	THE EMPEROR	123
2	B	THE WHEEL OF FORTUNE	206
3	C	THE MOON	90
4	D	THE DEVIL	85
5	E	THE HIEROPHANT	147
6	F	THE HIGH PRIESTESS	195
7	G	JUSTICE	87
8	H	THE HERMIT	106
9	I	THE MAGICIAN	90
10	J	THE WORLD	105

10 Letters   Sum Totals: 1,234

and $(1 + 2 + 3 + 4) = 10$

Moreover, the Alpha number of THE EMPEROR is 123, but when we add the *Tarot* number of his card to it (Tarot Key 4), we have the 123–4 in manifestation all over again in the letter A, the first letter of the English alphabet.

We can readily see that these Ten English Letters can easily be substituted for the Ten Tetractys in the Pythagorean symbol, especially since they add up to the number 1,234. But what about the Hebrew alphabet? Is there a similar substitution that can bring about the same effect in the Hebrew language?

The answer is, obviously, yes; and it is found in the *Tetra-grammaton*, the four Hebrew letters making up the Great Name for God (I H V H). These may be substituted for the Ten Tetractys in the following manner:

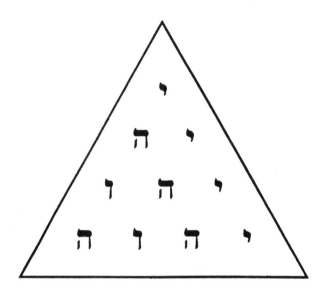

The Tetragrammaton of the Hebrews[9]

In this figure the 72 powers of the Great Name of God (I H V H) are brought into manifestation by following the example set by the Pythagoreans. It is to be noted that Hebrew words are read from right to left. The key to the problem is as follows:

Hebrew Letters		*Numerical Values*	
Apex Row	I	(10)	= 10
2nd Row	H I	(5 + 10)	= 15
3rd Row	V H I	(6 + 5 + 10)	= 21
4th Row	H V H I	(5 + 6 + 5 + 10)	= 26

The 72 Powers of the Great Name of God		= 72
Alpha Number for WORLD, the 10th English Letter J		= 72

Since everything in the final analysis is subservient to the principles of mathematics, even the four worlds of the Cabalah must be governed by the mathematical principles inherent in the four letters of the Tetragrammaton. For example: In the following figure is a diagram of these four cabalistic worlds in a circular format. AIN SOPH is the outer ring, and the four worlds of Atziluth, Briah, Yetzirah, and Assiah are contained within it. Yet Atziluth is very definitely controlled by the *Yod* (I), Briah by the *He* (H), Yetzirah by the *Vav* (V), and Assiah, the innermost and densest world of them all, by the

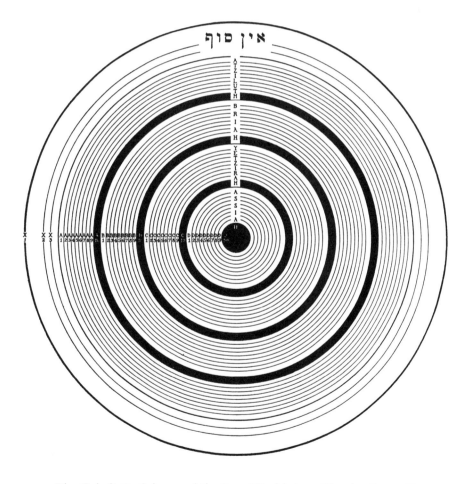

The Cabalistic Scheme of the Four Worlds in a Circular Format[9]

final *He* (H). The power or energy within each ring decreases as the Force travels inwards towards the center. Therefore, each outer ring controls those rings within it.

We see in the Tetragrammaton how important the Tetrad (the 4) is to the Decad (the 10). The sounds of the letters *Yod He Vav He* have been employed as a mantra for meditation by Cabalists down through the ages, or at least for the past 2,000 years, proving the importance that they gave to these Divine Names.

The Ten was also Pythagoras' symbol for the universe. Even in our own decimal system, it embraces all ten digits from the 0 to the 9. And it is Pythagoras who reminds us: "There is a mysterious connection between the gods and numbers, on which the science of arithmetic is based. The soul is a world that is self-moving; the soul contains in itself, and is, the quaternary, the tetractys."

One final thought before we bring this chapter to a close. In the following tabulation we have placed the four Hebrew letters for the word God on the left, as opposed to the three English letters for its equivalent word in English. The numerical values for the two systems are of course different.

Hebrew Letters and Number Values		English Letters and Alpha Numbers
Yod (I) = 10		
He (H) = 5		G = 7
Vav (V) = 6		O = 15
He (H) = 5		D = 4
26	Totals Are Equal	26

Yes, insofar as the English/Hebrew Cabalah is concerned, it could truly be said that one really does enhance the other.

NOTES

1. The diagram of the Sephirothic Tree of Life appearing in the first part of this chapter was translated from Kircher's *Oedipus Aegyptiacus,* Rome, 1652. It was taken from *The Secret Teachings of All Ages,* by Manly Palmer Hall (Los Angeles, Philosophical Research Society, 1928, 1978) page CXXIII

2. Ibid. Reproduced from an old Bible in *The Secret Teachings of All Ages,* by Manly Palmer Hall, page XCVIII

3. Ibid. Manly Palmer Hall, *The Secret Teachings of All Ages,* page XCVIII

4. The Star of David diagram for the Sephirothic Tree is from *Kabbalah, An Introduction and Illumination for the World Today,* by Charles Ponce (Wheaton, Illinois, The Theosophical Publishing House, 1973) page 102

5. All of the quotations from the *Sepher Yetzirah* appearing in this chapter are as translated by William Wynn Westcott (New York, Samuel Weiser, Inc., 1887, 1975)

6. The diagram of the modern version of the Sephirothic Tree is from one published by Paul Foster Case (Los Angeles, Builders of the Adytum, Ltd.)

7. For further information on the Qliphoth, the reader is referred to *The Mystical Qabalah,* by Dion Fortune (London, Williams and Norgate, Ltd., 1935, 1951) Chapter 26

8. Ibid. The diagram of the Four Sephirothic Trees was adapted from one in *The Secret Teachings of All Ages,* by Manly Palmer Hall, page CXXI

9. Ibid. For further informaton on the Tetractys, the Tetragrammaton, and the Four Worlds, the reader is referred to appropriate chapters in *The Secret Teachings of All Ages,* by Manly Palmer Hall. These illustrations originally appeared therein.

CHAPTER SIX

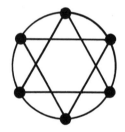

THE MYSTICAL LITERATURE

Those that give us food nourish our mortal body only,
those that entertain and instruct us in things of this world
enchant our lower minds alone, but those who awaken the
eternal spark within us, to them love and devotion are
ever due. [1]

—The Zohar

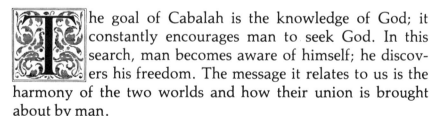he goal of Cabalah is the knowledge of God; it constantly encourages man to seek God. In this search, man becomes aware of himself; he discovers his freedom. The message it relates to us is the harmony of the two worlds and how their union is brought about by man.

Historians characterize Cabalah as an extremely sophisticated and enlightened philosophy, which, after thousands of years, teaches the deeply important distinction between *knowledge* and *wisdom*.

Cabalah is a unique phenomenon and may be considered mysticism, as it seeks an understanding of God and Creation whose intrinsic elements are beyond the grasp of the intellect. It is far removed from religion. It seems that mysticism takes its strength from deficiencies in religious practice. Essentially, the elements of Cabalah are perceived through contemplation and illumination. Some Cabalists have found the intellect itself to be a mystical phenomenon. Gershom Scholem, in his book *Kabbalah*, has written: "Mystical and esoteric elements coexist in Kabbalah in a highly confusing fashion. By its very nature, mysticism is knowledge that cannot be communicated directly but may be expressed only through symbol and metaphor. Esoteric knowledge, however, in theory can be transmitted, but those who possess it are either forbidden to pass it on, or do not wish to do so."[2]

In the earliest stages of its existence, the teaching of Cabalah was oral; hence the name QBLH, from QBL, meaning "to receive." It was then varied by the minds through which it filtered.

The origin of the Hebrew Cabalah is lost, but many declare it to have been brought down from Mount Sinai by Moses, who received it directly from God. Moses then transmitted it to seventy old men, and they in turn passed it on by word of mouth, until the time came when Ezra was commanded to transcribe it together with the Law. It eventually became accepted that Cabalah was the esoteric part of the "oral law" as given by Moses.

The earliest direct statement about Cabalah comes from the first century in the early Talmudic period. It was during this period that some of the main classics of Cabalah were written. These include the (1) *Heikhalot Books*, (2) *The Sepher Yetzirah* (Book of Formation), (3) *The Zohar* (Book of Splendor), and (4) *The Bahir* (Book of Brilliance).

The next section of this chapter deals with the ancient Hebrew mystical literature from which the Cabalah has its base. There are short examples following each subsection of how the original material appeared, translated into English.

The Heikhalot Books

Merkabah mysticism is the name given to the first chapter of Ezekiel. The term was used by Jewish mystics to designate the visions connected with the "Throne of Glory" and the "Chariot" (Merkabah). The doctrine of the seven heavens and

ADONAI

PITACORE

אדני

EZECHIEL

*The wheel of Pythagoras is a pentacle analogous to the
wheels of Ezekiel; the two emblems contain the same secrets
and belong to the same philosophy.*

—Eliphas Levi
Transcendental Magic

their Angelic Hosts is developed in Merkabah mysticism; it
has magical contexts. In the second century Christianity used
aspects of Merkabah mysticism conveyed from Jewish con-
verts. Part of the roots of Cabalah can be traced back to this
school of thought.

Rabbi Jochanan ben Zakkai was the father of Merkabah
mysticism and later traditions relate it to Rabbi Akiba and
Rabbi Ishmael. During the period of the Second Temple (538
B.C.E.–70 C.E.), this esoteric doctrine concerning the first chapter of Ezekiel was popular.

Most of these teachings are in scattered fragments, and only
a small portion is left to us today. The greater portion of these
teachings are in what is known as the *Heikhalot Books.*

The *Heikhalot Books* describe at great length the ascent of
the soul to heaven. They contain descriptions of heavenly
palaces or halls (Heikhalot), through which the mystic was
thought to pass on the way to the Merkabah. In the *Lesser
Heikhalot*, the principal speaker was Rabbi Akiba; this book
appears earlier in origin than the *Greater Heikhalot.*

The most famous *Heikhalot* book is the *Hebrew Book of
Enoch* (edited and translated into English in 1928 by Hugo
Odeburg).[4] The story this book tells is of the cobbler Enoch,
who, because he dedicated his life to piety, was taken by God
up to the heavens where he was turned into the first rank of
angels and was called Metatron. According to Eliphas Levi,
in his book *Transcendental Magic*, "Enoch is called Hermes by
the Egyptians; honored by the Phoenicians as Cadmus; author
of the sacred alphabet and the universal key to the initiations
of the Logos; and father of the Kabalah. Yet he, according to
sacred allegories, did not die like other men, but was trans-
ported to heaven, and will return at the end of time."

Levi continues: "Much the same parable is told of St. John
himself, who explained in his Apocalypse the symbolism of the
word of Enoch. This resurrection of St. John and Enoch,
expected at the close of the ages of ignorance, will be the reno-

vation of their doctrine by the comprehension of the kabalistic keys which unlock the temple of unity and of universal philosophy, too long occult (hidden) and reserved solely for the elect, who perish at the hands of the world."[5] It seems we are now moving into this time frame that Eliphas Levi speaks of.

In addition to interpretations and visions based on Merkabah mysticism, other esoteric traditions began to crystallize around the first chapter of Genesis, which was called *Maaseh Berashith* or the History of Creation. During the period of the Second Temple (538 B.C.E.–C.E.), the esoteric teachings concerning the first chapter of Genesis and the first chapter of Ezekiel were prevalent.

In the *Book of Splendours*, Eliphas Levi explains: "The Bible gives man two names: the first is Adam, which means 'drawn from the earth,' or 'man of earth'; the second is Enos or Enoch, which means 'divine man,' or 'lifted to God.'

"According to Genesis, it is Enoch who first spoke publicly on the principle of beings (two) and this same Enoch was, it is said, taken alive up into heaven after having engraved the primitive elements of religion and universal science on two stones which are called the columns or pillars of Enoch.

"This Enoch is not a person, but a personification of humanity, uplifted by religion and science to a sense of immortality. At the time designated by the name of Enoch, the cult of God appears on earth and ritual worship begins. This time also marks the beginning of civilization with writing and the hieratic movements."

Eliphas Levi goes on to say, "Who would believe that the book which inspired all these theories and religious symbols has been preserved, coming down to us in the form of a deck of strange cards? Nothing is truer, however, and Court de Gebelin, since followed by all those who have seriously studied the symbolism of these cards, was the first to discover it, in the last century."[6] Levi is referring, of course, to the deck of Tarot cards.

The Vision of Ezekiel is the central fable of Merkabah mysticism, from the "Bear" Bible. This plate shows the Merkabah, or chariot of Jehovah, which appeared to Ezekiel by the river Chebar. [3]

The discovery of the Dead Sea Scrolls in 1947 and the literary remains of the Qumran sect show such ideas as the Merkabah were known among them. Merkabah terminology was found in a hymn fragment where angels praise "the image of the Throne of the Chariot." This fragment has now been translated and published by J. Strugnell in his paper, *The Angelic Liturgy at Qumran.*[7] The Qumran sect possessed the original *Book of Enoch*, both in Hebrew and Aramaic.

The Merkabah (Chariot) as It Is Depicted in the Tarot

The word *Merkabah* means "Chariot" in English, and it is shown in the above reproduction of the 7th Tarot card of the Major Arcana. These Merkabah teachings were some of the earliest teachings of Cabalah, and it is quite significant that we should see them return again in the symbology of the Tarot.

An interesting observation: The great "I AM" is that which was in the beginning. And since the Alpha number for "I AM" is 23, its symbol would be the letter W, the symbol of the Chariot (Tarot card 7). This is the Merkabah, the vehicle for the soul's ascent into heaven. Therefore, by the use of Gematria, the following relationships become known:

$$I\ AM = (9 + 1 + 13) = 23 = W$$
$$W = THE\ CHARIOT = (33 + 74) = 107$$
$$CABALAH\ PRIMER = (28 + 79) = 107$$

We can only conclude, then, that *Cabalah Primer*, the title of this beginning book of Cabalah, could quite possibly offer an assist in the same manner as the Chariot, and thereby enable the reader to ascend once more into the Higher Consciousness.

The following is a translation of the *Greater Heikhalot*, from Aryeh Kaplan's book on *Meditation and Kabbalah*. Here is an example of one of its twenty-six chapters.

Chapter I:
"Rabbi Ishmael said: What is the meaning of the hymns that one must chant when he desires to gaze into a vision of the *Merkava* (Merkabah), to descend in peace and to ascend in peace?

"When one is on a higher level, he can enter, and is brought in and led to the heavenly Chambers, where he is allowed to stand before the Throne of Glory. He then knows what will happen in the future, who will be raised and who will be lowered, who will be made strong and who will be cut off, who will be made poor and who will be made rich, who will die and who will live, who will have his inheritance taken from him, and who will have it given to him, who will be invested with the Torah, and who will be given wisdom.

"When one is on a (still) higher level, he can see all the secret deeds of man. He knows and recognizes the adulterer, the murderer, and the one who is only suspected of these things. All this he knows and recognizes.

"When one is on a (still) higher level, he knows all kinds of sorcery.

"When one is on a (still) higher level, whoever raises his hand to strike him is clothed in leprosy. . . .

"When one is on a (still) higher level, whoever speaks against him maliciously is taken and cast down. He is dealt severe blows, and suffers from infected wounds.

"When one is on a (still) higher level, he is separated from all men, and distinguished from all humanity by his traits. He is honored by those on earth and by those on high. Whoever sins against him, sins greatly, and evil falls upon him from heaven. Whoever casts a hand against him, suffers retribution by the hand of the heavenly tribunal."[8]

The Sepher Yetzirah

The *Sepher Yetzirah,* or Book of Formation, is the oldest treatise of Judaism. It is attributed by legend to Abraham the Patriarch. The *Sepher Yetzirah* was recorded in the second century. The final chapter of the *Sepher Yetzirah* reveals plainly that its creation was the result of a visionary experience. Attention given *Yetzirah* by prominent scholars helped to establish it and its mystical views and ideas that became basic to Cabalah. Besides being a standard text for Jewish mystics, *Yetzirah* influenced Christian Cabalists.

It is a short but enigmatic work consisting altogether of some 2,000 words, which has baffled scholars through the centuries. Several editions of the English translation have been published. The work explains the mystery of creation, drawing parallels between the origin of the world, the sun, the planets, the elements, seasons, and man.

The work further explains the "thirty-two paths of wisdom" which are defined as ten Sephiroth or primordial numbers, and the twenty-two letters of the Hebrew alphabet. The term "path" is used throughout the Hebrew Cabalah to signify a hieroglyphical idea. The *Sepher Yetzirah* is a numerical treatise on the origin of the universe.

In W. Wynn Westcott's translation of the *Sepher Yetzirah*, he quotes Eliphas Levi, the famous French occultist, who wrote in his *History of Magic:* "The *Zohar* is a Genesis of illumination, the *Sepher Jezirah* (Yetzirah) is a ladder formed of truths. Therein are explained the thirty-two absolute signs of sounds, numbers, and letters: each letter reproduces a number, an idea, and a form; so that mathematics are capable of application to ideas and to forms not less rigorously than to numbers, by exact proportion and perfect correspondence. By the science of the *Sepher Jezirah* (Yetzirah) the human spirit is fixed to truth, and in reason, and is able to take account of the possible development of intelligence by the evolutions of numbers. The *Zohar* represents absolute truth, and the *Sepher Jezirah* (Yetzirah) provides the means by which we may seize, appropriate, and make use of it."[9]

The *Sepher Yetzirah* reflects the very essence of the Cabalah itself. But it is still not understood in its entirety because mankind today has failed to grasp the single thread that ties the whole to its infinite number of parts. "What is that?" you ask. The answer lies in the "Unwritten Cabalah," that part of the Law that was considered so sacred that it was never put into writing, but only communicated orally from Teacher to disciple. Yet, even though he was forbidden to reveal the Law in its entirety, the author of the *Sepher Yetzirah* still gives us enough hints as to what this Universal Law actually is, and it seems incredible that it still remains hidden, at least to the outer world.

The following quotation explains how *Phi* is brought into manifestation, simply by following the commandments in the *Sepher Yetzirah*. (For those who want to dig and understand more regarding the *Book of Formation*, I would recommend William Eisen's *The Essence of the Cabalah.*)

These are direct quotations from the *Sepher Yetzirah*, first chapter, verses 3 and 4, as translated by W. Wynn Westcott:[10]

(1:3) "The ineffable Sephiroth are Ten, so are the Numbers; and as there are in man five fingers over against five, so over them is established a covenant of strength, by word of mouth, and by the circumcision of the flesh."

(1:4) "Ten is the number of the ineffable Sephiroth, ten and not nine, ten and not eleven. Understand this wisdom, and be wise in the perception. Search out concerning it, restore the Word to its creator, and replace Him who formed it upon his throne."

We can clearly see that the author of the *Sepher Yetzirah* pleads with you to look at this covenant, and understand the basic principles of *Phi.* The way the fingers are put together gives the Phi proportion, as illustrated on the following page. The fingers form a decagon which is the perfect Phi proportion between the radius and its sides, and it gives you the universal symbol. Every lineal increment within a decagon also makes a Phi proportion with every other increment; that is, each rib is an individual term in the great Phi sequence of numbers.

Here we find, to our absolute astonishment and amazement, that the one Universal Law that the ancient rabbis considered so sacred that they never committed it to writing, was none other than the Phi Law, the Golden Mean, the Divine Proportion. This, then, is the reason that there are ten Sephiroth and not nine, ten and not eleven, for the only way that the Golden number Phi can be brought into manifestation is by placing exactly *ten* Sephiroth in a circle, no more and no less, around a central core. Yes, the ancient Hebrew priests understood Phi and they plead with us to understand this wisdom: "Search out concerning it," they say, "and restore the Word to its creator."

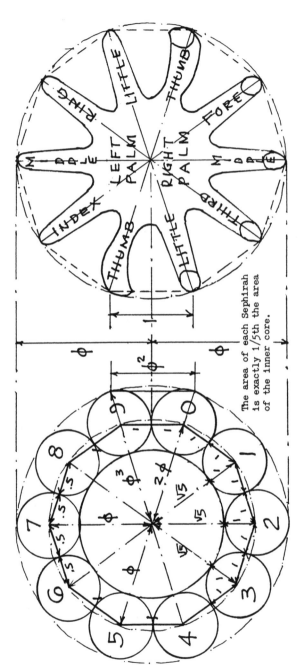

The area of each Sephirah is exactly 1/5th the area of the inner core.

(I: 3) THE INEFFABLE SEPHIROTH ARE TEN, SO ARE THE NUMBERS; AND AS THERE ARE IN MAN FIVE FINGERS OVER AGAINST FIVE, SO OVER THEM IS ESTABLISHED A COVENANT OF STRENGTH, BY WORD OF MOUTH, AND BY THE CIRCUMCISION OF THE FLESH.

(I: 4) TEN IS THE NUMBER OF THE INEFFABLE SEPHIROTH, TEN AND NOT NINE, TEN AND NOT ELEVEN. UNDERSTAND THIS WISDOM, AND BE WISE IN THE PERCEPTION. SEARCH OUT CONCERNING IT, RESTORE THE WORD TO ITS CREATOR, AND REPLACE HIM WHO FORMED IT UPON HIS THRONE.

How Phi Is Brought into Manifestation by Following the Commandments in the Sepher Yetzirah (Book of Formation)

The Zohar

The *Zohar*, also called the "Book of Splendor" or the "Book of Light," is a collection of many separate writings on Deity, Angels, Souls, and Cosmogony. It is the most influential book in the history of Jewish mysticism. Its author is said to be Rabbi Simeon ben Yohai, who lived around 160 A.D. Considerable portions of the work may have been arranged by him from the oral traditions of his time, and other parts have certainly been added by other hands at various intervals, but he is the one to whom the original writing is accredited. It was first published as a whole by Rabbi Moses de Leon, of Guadalajara, Spain, in 1290 A.D.

The *Zohar* is a collection of treatises that are considerably different from one another in their external form. Most of the *Zohar* seems to be interpretations of biblical passages artfully composed in which Rabbi Simeon, otherwise known as the "Sacred Light," and his disciples and friends interpret the words of Scripture in accordance with their hidden meaning. Many sections even appear as *fragments of oracles* and *reports of* actual secret revelations.

Yet the contributors to the *Zohar* presented their ideas in the most obscure and least logical way, sometimes going so far as to use biblical commentary as a support for some very abtruse conclusions. Therefore, it is important for us to understand just what they really meant in their interpretation of these sacred Scriptures. And in the same way that the *Zohar* provided spiritual insights into the Pentateuch or the five books of Moses (the proper Zohar is a commentary on these books), so can the Cabalah provide us with an insight into the *Zohar*.

These are the reasons that the *Zohar* is regarded as that book in which the most varied and often contradictory forces of the Cabalistic movement are to be found. But at the close of the Talmudic period, it became all but unknown except in small secret groups. Then it came to light again in the late 13th century, when Moses de Leon published it in its entirety. And since that time, the *Zohar*, that great classic of Cabalah, has become the most studied and one of the most important books of them all. Teachings of other schools were soon forgotten, as Cabalists tried to unravel the mysteries of this ancient book.

The *Zohar* says: "And ye shall know that I am the LORD your God." (Zohar II: 25a). The start and the goal of the *Zohar* is knowledge of God. Cabalah encourages man to constantly seek God, the "beginning and the end of all things." Man, by means of this search, then becomes aware of himself and obtains his own freedom.

The following selection is quoted directly from the *Zohar*, in order that the reader might examine the style and great wisdom of its words. It was edited and translated by Gershom Scholem.[11]

The Hidden Meaning of the Torah

"Rabbi Simeon said: If a man looks upon the Torah as merely a book presenting narratives and everyday matters, alas for him! Such a torah, one treating with everyday concerns, and indeed a more excellent one, we too, even we, could compile. More than that, in the possession of the rulers of the world there are books of even greater merit, and these we could emulate if we wished to compile some such torah. But the Torah, in all of its words, holds supernal truths and sublime secrets.

"See how precisely balanced are the upper and the lower worlds. Israel here below is balanced by the angels on high, concerning whom it stands written: "who makest thy angels into winds" (Psalms 104:4). For when the angels descend to earth they don earthly garments, else they could neither abide in the world, nor could it bear to have them. But if this is so with the angels, then how much more so it must be with the Torah: the Torah it was that created the angels and created all the worlds and through Torah are all sustained. The world could not endure the Torah if she had not garbed herself in garments of this world.

"Thus the tales related in the Torah are simply her outer garments, and woe to the man who regards that outer garb as the Torah itself, for such a man will be deprived of portion in the next world. Thus David said: "Open Thou mine eyes, that I may behold wondrous things out of Thy law" (Psalms 119:18), that is to say, the things that are underneath. See now. The most visible part of a man are the clothes that he has on, and they who lack understanding, when they look at the man, are apt not to see more in him than these clothes. In reality, however, it is the body of the man that constitutes the pride of his clothes, and his soul constitutes the pride of his body.

"So it is with the Torah. Its narrations which relate to the things of the world constitute the garments which clothe the body of the Torah; and that body is composed of the Torah's precepts, gufey-torah (bodies, major principles). People without understanding see only the narrations, the garment; those somewhat more penetrating see also the body. But the truly wise, those who serve the most high King and stood on mount Sinai, pierce all the way through to the soul, to the true Torah which is the root principle of all. These same will in the future be vouchsafed to penetrate to the very soul of the soul of the Torah.

"See now how it is like this in the highest world, with garment, body, soul and super-soul. The outer garments are the heavens and all therein, the body is the Community of Israel and it is the recipient of the soul, that is 'the Glory of Israel'; and the soul of the soul is the Ancient Holy One. All of these are conjoined one within the other.

"Woe to the sinners who look upon the Torah as simply tales pertaining to things of the world, seeing thus only the outer garment. But the righteous whose gaze penetrates to the very Torah, happy are they. Just as wine must be in a jar to keep, so the Torah must be contained in an outer garment. That garment is made up of the tales and stories; but we, we are bound to penetrate beyond."[11]

—The Zohar

The Bahir

The *Bahir* in its entirety is a very small book, thirty to forty pages long, no more than 12,000 words; but its statements altered the course of Jewish mysticism.

Like the *Zohar*, at the close of the Talmudic period, the *Bahir* (Book of Brilliance) became almost unknown. It came to light again in Provence, France, during the 13th century.

At this time, the literature again inspired individuals to teach the secret mysteries, and the *Bahir* began to be openly taught.

The primary importance of the *Bahir* is that (1) it contains the theory of *Gilgul* or reincarnation, (2) it uses symbolic language and explains the *Sephiroth*, and (3) it identifies the feminine principle in God in the *Shekhinah*, a divine entity, a portion of God himself, but as a feminine power.

It is one of the oldest Cabalistic texts. It is in this book we have the earliest discussion of the Sephiroth used to form a bridge between God and the Universe.

The *Zohar* was published in approximately 1295 A.D., and until that time the *Bahir* was the most important classical Cabalah text. But there are passages in the *Zohar* which expound upon the concepts of the *Bahir*. There is a similarity in both works: the *Bahir* is called Book of Brilliance, and the *Zohar*, Book of Light—this is interesting, both of the books refer to Light.

An important concept of the *Bahir* is Tzimtzum (the self-constriction of God's Light). This concept proposes that in the beginning God first "withdrew" His Light, forming a vacant space in which creation could take place. Then God drew a *thread* of His Light through this empty space, thus enabling the creative processes to begin. The space is dark to us; but to God, all is Light.

Aryeh Kaplan has written that the clearest statement of the Tzimtzum can be found in the writings of Rabbi Isaac Luria

(1534–1572), known as the Ari, who headed the Saded school of Kabbalah. As described in "Etz Chaim" (Tree of Life), the process was as follows:

> "Before all things were created . . . the Supernal Light was simple, and it filled all existence. There was no empty space . . .
>
> "When His simple Will decided to create all universes . . . He constricted the Light to the sides . . . leaving a vacant space . . . This space was perfectly round. . . .
>
> "After this constriction took place . . . there was a place in which all things could be created . . . He then drew a single straight thread from the Infinite Light . . . and brought it into that vacated space . . . It was through that line that the Infinite Light was brought down below. . . ."[12]

In doing some research on Cabalah, I happened to open Aryeh Kaplan's excellent translation of the *Bahir*, part of which is quoted above. In the first paragraph of his introduction he ascribed the *Bahir* to *Rabbi Nehuniah ben Hakana*, a Talmudic sage of the first century. The reason for this is that Rabbi Nehuniah is the sage who opens the text, as well as the fact that he was known to be the leader of a major mystical school that flourished in the Holy Land. Aside from this tradition, however, there would be little internal evidence in the text to support this attribution. After the first paragraph his name is never mentioned again in the text. But Aryeh Kaplan writes: "An interesting possibility is that *Rabbi Amorai*, who plays an important role in the *Bahir*, is actually a pseudonym for *Rabbi Nehuniah*." He goes on to say "careful study indicates that this mysterious Rabbi Amorai, who is mentioned nine times in the text, is actually the source of the main teachings found in the *Bahir*."[13]

This is a good opportunity to see what the Cabalah can tell us about these two rabbis. Let us first spell out their names as they are normally spelled in English, and then compare their Alpha numbers.

```
R A B B I    N E H U N I A H    B E N    H A K A N A
18-1-2-2-9   14-5-8-21-14-9-1-8  2-5-14   8-1-11-1-14-1
   32      +       80        +   21  +      36       = 169


R A B B I    A M O R A I
18-1-2-2-9   1-13-15-18-1-9
   32      +      57       = 89
```

RABBI NEHUNIAH BEN HAKANA = 169
RABBI AMORAI   = 89
_____
             Difference   = 80

When subtracted the balance is equal to *80,* the alpha number for *NEHUNIAH.* It seems that Aryeh Kaplan is correct in his assumption. The Cabalah tells us that Rabbi Amorai could very well have been Rabbi Nehuniah ben Hakana.

The following are two selections from the *Bahir* which were edited by Rebven Margaliot in Hebrew, and then translated into English by Zion Bokser in his book *The Mystical Tradition.* They deal with the subject of reincarnation. The text reads as follows:

1. "Why is it that there is a righteous person who enjoys good, and there is a righteous person who suffers affliction? It is because in the latter case that righteous person was formerly wicked, and he is now suffering punishment. But is one punished for offenses committed during one's youth? Did not R. Simon say that the heavenly tribunal inflicts punishment only for misdeeds committed after the twentieth year of a person's life? He replied to him: I do not refer to misdeeds in the course

of the person's life. I refer to the fact that that person pre-existed prior to his present life. His colleagues said to him: How long will you mystify your statement? He said to them: Consider the analogy to the person who planted vines in his garden and he hoped that they would grow good grapes, but they grew bad grapes. He realized that he had not succeeded. He did a new planting, fenced it in, after he had cleared out the bad vine. He planted a second time but saw he had not succeeded. He fenced it in, did a new planting after he cleaned out the bad vine. He saw that he had not succeeded and he plucked out the bad vine and did a new planting. How long does this go on? He said to them: For a thousand generations, as it is written (Ps. 105:8): 'The matter which He ordained for a thousand generations.' (Sefer haBahir 195)"

2. "What is the significance of the phrase "from generation to generation" (Ps. 106:10)? Said R. Pappias: It alludes to the verse (Ecclesiastes 1:4): "One generation goes and one generation comes" (ba, which also means "came"), on which Rabbi Akiva commented: It is the same generation which came before. To what may this be compared? To the king who had servants whom he robed, in accordance with his means, in finely embroidered silk garments. But they misbehaved. He rejected them and took off their garments, and they departed. He took the garments and washed them well until they were without stain, and he kept them in readiness. He acquired new servants and robed them in those garments, without knowing whether those servants would be good or bad. Thus they acquired garments which had been used previously and others had worn before them. But the earth abides forever, and this is the meaning of the verse (Ecclesiastes 12:7): 'The dust returns to the earth as it was, but the spirit returns to God who gave it.' (ibid. 121, 122)"[14]

NOTES

1. Quotation from the *Zohar* taken from *The Mysteries of the Qabalah* (Chicago, Ill., The Yogi Publication Society, 1922) last page

2. Gershom Scholem, *Kabbalah* (Jerusalem, Keter Publishing House, Ltd., 1974) page 4

3. Manly Palmer Hall, *The Secret Teachings of All Ages* (Los Angeles, Philosophical Research Society, 1928, 1978) page CXXV

4. Edited and translated by Hugo Odenburg, *The Hebrew Book of Enoch or 3 Enoch* (England, University Press, 1928)

5. Eliphas Levi, *Transcendental Magic* (New York, Samuel Weiser, 1974) page 43

6. Eliphas Levi, *The Book of Splendours* (New York, Samuel Weiser, 1973) page 136

7. J. Strugnell, paper called The Angelic Liturgy at Qumran, Supplements to *Vetus Testamentum*, Vol. VII (Oxford, congress volume, 1959, Leiden 1060) pages 318–345

8. Aryeh Kaplan, *Meditation and Kabbalah* (York Beach, Maine, Samuel Weiser, Inc., 1982) page 42

9. William Wynn Westcott, *Sepher Yetzirah, The Book of Formation and the Thirty-two Paths of Wisdom*, translated from the Hebrew (New York, Samuel Weiser, first printed 1887, revised 1893, reprinted 1975) page 7

10. Ibid. William Wynn Westcott, Sepher Yetzirah, page 15

11. Edited by Gershom G. Scholem, *Zohar—The Book of Splendor, Basic Readings from the Kabbalah* (New York, Schocken Books, 1949) pages 121–122

12. Aryeh Kaplan, *The Bahir* (New York, Samuel Weiser, Inc., 1979) pages xiii–xiv Quotation translated by Aryeh Kaplan to English from Rabbi Isaac Luria, Etz Chaim (Tree of Life)

13. Ibid. Aryeh Kaplan, *The Bahir*, introduction pages iii–iv

14. Ben Zion Bokser, *The Hebrew Mystical Tradition* (New York, The Pilgrim Press, 1981). Selection from the *Bahir* was edited by Reuvin Margoliot in Hebrew, then by Ben Zion Bokser to English, page 84

CHAPTER SEVEN

CABALISTIC PRACTICES OF CONTEMPLATION
AND MEDITATION

Everyday below is controlled by a day above. Now an act below stimulates a corresponding activity above. Thus if a man does kindness on earth, he awakens loving kindness above, and it rests upon that day which is crowned therewith through him. Similarly if he performs a deed of mercy, he crowns that day with mercy and it becomes his protector in the hour of need. [1]

—Zohar III, page 92a

abalah deals with many new "ideas." Yet we must find practical application for what we learn here.

"When will the Messiah come?" asked Rabbi Simeon of the prophet Elijah who often came down from heaven to speak with the master of the Zohar. "This very day," answered the prophet. "Go to the gate of Rome and you will see." Rabbi Simeon went to the gate of Rome, remained there all day, then came away, having seen nothing more than a number of beggars covered with sores and a stranger, poor in appearance, who consoled them and ministered to their wounds. Once home, he found Elijah there and said, "Master, why have you mocked your servant?" "But I have not deceived," said the prophet. "Did you not see a man

"The Soul as Guide, Showing the Way," Watercolor by William Blake for Dante's Purgatorio, Canto IV.

performing works of charity? Well, I say to you that the reign of charity is the Messiah's reign, and if you wish for the coming of the Messiah everyday, then perform charity everyday."

Eliphas Levi clarifies it even further by stating: "Charity according to the Apostle St. John, is the substance and final goal of Christianity. Charity will outlast unfulfilled prophecies and outmoded knowledge. Charity in the words of the same apostle, is greater than hope and faith."[2]

Yet charity does not mean just helping an old lady across a street. It means fulfilling the inner goals your soul has set for you in this life. Goodness is certainly part of this. The old saying "charity begins at home" has real meaning; it means start by doing what is correct for your Inner Self (your home). Meditation and contemplation are tools used by Cabalists to help get in touch with their act of "charity" or their inner self.

Cabalah is discussed in many volumes of writing, but all the teachings are not encased in the written words of books. Inner devotion, prayer, contemplation, meditation are emphasized in preparing man for knowledge about the upper world and refining his soul so he can be drawn upward or absorbed into the hidden life of the Godhead.

C. G. Jung has indicated that the word *meditation* is used when a person has an inner dialogue with someone unseen. It may be with God, when He is invoked, or with himself, or with a good angel. Meditation is an inner dialogue and hence a living relationship to the answering voice of the "other" in ourselves.

The greatest Cabalists were Masters of mystical prayer; they understood that the soul talks to us in symbols. The actual text of prayer serves as a kind of banister which the Cabalist holds as he makes his ascent; he transforms words of the prayer that serve as landmarks on the upward climb.

Three main styles of contemplative practices were used by the early Cabalists: (1) the Letters, using the alphabet and letter permutation; (2) the Spheres, using the Tree of Life; (3) Ecstasy, using dance, swaying, singing, and humor.

In the following subsections are some small descriptions of methods used at various periods of Cabalistic history.

Meditation as Described in the Greater Heikhalot

The earliest statement regarding meditation came from the early Talmudic period, the first century after the destruction of Solomon's Temple. This was the age of the prophets. The Cabalists of this period engaged in meditative techniques to attain spiritual elevation and to transcend the worldly materialistic realm. Techniques consisted of the repetition of Divine Names, as well as intense concentration on the spheres or Tree of Life. What we know of these early first century methods comes down to us in the *Greater Heikhalot* Book.

It was during this period that some of the main classics of Cabalah were written. These include the *Sepher Yetzirah*, the *Zohar* and the *Bahir*. The mysteries contained within them were taught individually to one worthy disciple at a time. These secrets were entrusted only to the religious leaders of each generation.

The *Greater Heikhalot* Book explicitly describes the methods through which one enters the mystical state. The key appears to be a meditation where a series of Divine Names is repeated 112 times. Through repetition of these Divine Names, one enters the threshold of the mystical chamber, and then proceeds from one chamber to the next. In this process a precise knowledge of the names of the angels, and the various formulas of the names of seals is needed to ascend from one chamber to another. Ascending through the chambers is like a spiritual projection; one ascends mentally, not physically. (For greater detail of this method I would recommend Aryeh Kaplan's book called *Meditation and Kabbalah*).[3]

When the initiate reaches the step before the seventh and final chamber, he is placed in a *Chariot*. This type of mystical experience is called *Merkabah*, which means *Chariot*. The *Merkabah* is a spiritual vehicle that one creates for himself, which enables him to ascend into the mystical state.

Meditation as Described by Rabbi Abraham Abulafia

One of the most colorful figures in early cabalistic history was Rabbi Abraham Abulafia of Spain (1240 A.D.) with his *Prophetic Kabbalah.*

He refashioned the mystical discipline and made use of the letters of the alphabet, and especially of the Tetragrammaton and other names of God, *to empty his mind* of all natural forms that might prevent his concentration on divine matters. In this way, *he freed his mind and soul* of natural restraints and *opened it to divine input* and the possible attainment of prophecy. Rabbi Abulafia was thoroughly familiar with the mystical works from the Talmudical period, such as the *Bahir* which in his opinion was the greatest of all cabalistic texts.

The *Sepher Yetzirah* played a major role in the turning point of his life. Abulafia writes that his introduction to the *Sepher Yetzirah* became his initiation into the mysteries.

Abulafia describes what the obstacles and dangers, as well as the rewards, of these mystical experiences could bring.

He wrote about the "science of combination" and music, which could also take the soul to a state of the highest rapture by the combination of sounds. Breathing exercises, the repetition of the Divine Names, meditation on colors were techniques of *Prophetic Kabbalah* used to aid the ascent of the soul. These techniques bear a very definite resemblance to those of Indian Yoga or Muslim Sufism. The subject sees flashes of light and feels that he has made identification with an inner spiritual Guru, or sometimes the subject's own Higher Self. This was the object of Abulafia's Prophetic Kabbalism, the union of the devotee with his spiritual master.

An example is the Tetragrammaton. There are 24 (1 × 2 × 3 × 4) possible permutations or rearrangements of the letters in the Divine Name *Yod He Vav He* (YHVH). But when you rearrange the *order* in which the permutations themselves are made, you can find many more. Abulafia gives us the following list for our contemplation:

PERMUTATIONS OF THE TETRAGRAMMATON
(R. Abraham Ben Samuel Abulafia)[5]

YHVH	YHHV	YVHH	YVHH	HVHY	HVYH
HVHV	HVYH	HHYV	HHYV	VHYH	VHHY
VHYH	VHHY	VYHH	VYHH	HYHV	HYVH
HYHV	HYVH	HHVY	HHVY	YHVH	YHHV
YHHV	YVHH	HVHY	HVHY	HVYH	HHYV
HVYH	HHYV	VHYH	VHYH	VHHY	VYHH
VHHY	VYHH	HYHV	HYHV	HYVH	HHVY
HYVH	HHVY	YHVH	YHVH	YHHV	YVHH
HVYH	HHYV	VHYH	VHYH	VHHY	VYHH
VHHY	VYHH	HYVH	HYVH	HYVH	HHVY
HYVH	HHVY	YHVH	YHVH	YHHV	YVHH
YHHV	YVHH	HVHY	HVHY	HVHY	HHYV
HHYV	HVYH	VHHY	VHHY	VYHH	HYHV
VYHH	HYHV	HYVH	HYVH	HHVY	YHVH
HHVY	YHVH	YHHV	YHHV	YVHH	HVHY
YVHH	HVHY	HVYH	HVYH	HHYV	VHYH
VYHH	HYHV	HYVH	HYVH	HHVY	YHVH
HHVY	YHVH	YHHV	YHHV	YVHH	HVHY
YVHH	HVHY	HVYH	HVYH	HHYV	VHYH
HHYV	VHYH	VHHY	VHHY	VYHH	HYHV
HYHV	HYVH	HHVY	HHVY	YHVH	YHHV
YHVH	YHHV	YVHH	YVHH	HVHY	HVYH
HVHY	HVYH	HHYV	HHYV	VHYH	VHHY
VHYH	VHHY	VYHH	VYHH	HYHV	HYVH

Note: the 10th Hebrew letter *Yod* is spelled in English by the letters J, I, or Y, depending on individual preferences. There is no "standard" method of English nomenclature for these Hebrew letters.

Quoting Ben Zion Bokser in his book *The Jewish Mystical Tradition:* "Abulafia introduced an ascetic as well as an ecstatic influence into the Kabbalah. His basic concern was to chart a way of liberating man from the 'knots' and 'seals' that keep him in a kind of imprisonment in the world of sense experience. The way of liberation was to withdraw from mundane affairs, from the world of flux, into the world of the intellect, so that the soul might be free to reunite itself with the Active Intellect, with God who is the reality behind the phenomenal world. This concept was close to the teachings of Maimonides, and, indeed, Abulafia was an ardent Maimonidean all his life.

"While starting with Maimonidean rationalism he went beyond it. True liberation can be attained only by another type of meditation. The contemplation of the conceptual world for Abulafia still left one in the realm of finitude. To go beyond, to reach the eternal flow of divine energy pulsating through the universe and emanating from beyond it, he advocated meditating on the letters of the Hebrew alphabet, in their various permutations and combinations in their relationship to the names of God. The highest reward that would come to the mystic pursuing this path was the attainment of prophecy."[4]

Meditation as Described in the "Gates of Light"

Even though the most important teaching of Hebrew Cabalah involves the ten Sephiroth, it is surprising to find they rarely appear in cabalistic literature on meditation. In general, the early writing on meditation says little about the ten Sephiroth.

There was one exception to this; it was the remarkable book by Rabbi Joseph Gikatilla called *Gates of Light.* Joseph Gikatilla, born in Castile, 1248 A.D., was considered one of the greatest Cabalists of his period. He studied under Abraham Abulafia.

The *Gates of Light* is a treatise of the ten Sephiroth and the ten Divine Names that are associated with these spheres. It is considered by many to be the key to the mystical teachings of the *Bahir.*

According to Gershom Scholem, a great Hebrew scholar, the *Gates of Light* is a detailed explanation of cabalistic symbolism and the designations of the ten Sephiroth, starting with

Title page of "Portae Lucis," a Latin translation by Paulus Ricius of J. Gikatilla, "Sha'arei Orah" (Gates of Light), Augsburg, 1516. Pictured is a man holding a tree with the ten Sephiroth.

the last, and going on up to the highest.[6] This book is a guide to meditation, and it teaches one to ascend spiritually on the ladder of the Sephiroth of the Tree of Life. The Tree is a primary image to raise ourselves to higher perceptions. Today we call this kind of meditation "guided imagery," using the Sephiroth to correspond to the various parts of our body, and then seeing white light going up and down it as in the Tree. *Therefore to meditate on the Tree of Life, we find that within ourselves we have a great filing cabinet in which we may sort and store knowledge as we receive it.*

The adept of Cabalah must experience and master all things in order to achieve supreme perfection and power. The Tree of Life is a statement of the belief that man is a miniature replica of the universe and God, and that he is capable of spiritually expanding himself to become God. The Tree of the ten Sephiroth is believed to be a cosmic diagram.

Meditation as Described by Rabbi Isaac Luria, the Ari

Aryeh Kaplan has written in his book *Meditation and Kabbalah* that "there is a select number of individuals who live on a plane so high above the rest of humanity that it seems as if they are completely different, higher species of being. They teach, but we grasp but little, and from the few crumbs that we glean, we can build mountains. Such a person was Rabbi Isaac Luria (1534–1572 A.D.), renowned as the greatest Kabbalist of modern times. Rabbi Isaac Luria is commonly known as the Ari, an acronym standing for "Elohi Rabbi Isaac"—the Godly Rabbi Isaac. No other master or sage ever had this extra letter, standing for—Elohi—Godly—prefaced to his name."[7]

The Ari was born in Jerusalem, studied in Egypt, and settled in Safed (Palestine) where he studied Cabalah with Moses Cordovero for a short time until Cordovero's death. It was here in Safed where he began to impart his original cabalistic systems to a number of students. His student, Hayyim Vital, later recorded the Ari's work. The most famous works recorded were *Eight Gates* and *The Gates of the Holy Spirit*.

The most important system of meditation the Ari developed

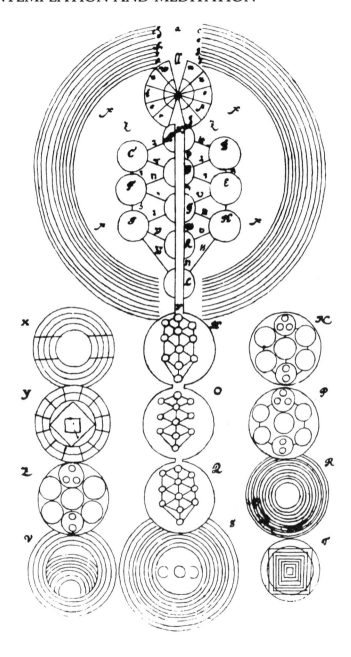

Chart showing the gradual development of the Sephiroth, according to Lurianic Cabalah. From Knorr von Rosenroth, "Kabbala Denudata," Frankfort, 17th century. [9]

was called "Yichudim" or "Acts of Unifications." This is a practice where one manipulates the letters of various names of God or the Tetragrammaton. According to Aryeh Kaplan, "The word itself indicates a unification, and in general, these names are intertwined and various vowel points are added. Since the various divine Names reflect spiritual forces, and the forces have their counterparts in different parts of the human mind, these Yichudim (or Unifications) can have a powerful effect in the integrating of the psyche."[8] "Hear O Israel, the Lord is our God, the Lord is One": this is a unification of a name.

Many of the Ari's meditations were for specific purposes, like the rectification of sins; or for esoteric rites, such as exorcism and to seek enlightenment. Isaac Luria was in the habit of giving each of his disciples one of these unifications in accordance with the root of his soul. This sounds like the mantra we might be given today by a Yoga Master.

Meditation as Described in the Hasidic Movement

In the late 18th century (the golden period of the Hasidic movement) descriptions, once again, are recorded of the mystical nature in meditation.

Hasidism captured the popular imagination as no other mystical movement before it. It was its meditative practices that gave Hasidism its great impetus.

The Hasidic movement was founded by Rabbi Israel, better known as Baal Shem Tov (1698–1760 A.D.). Where Cabalah before was only for the learning of the more advanced scholars, it had now become part of the popular folklore. One of the Baal Shem Tov's most important contributions was to give a safe method of meditation which could be used by simple people.

The focal point was to repeat the "Amidah" (silent portion of daily prayer) three times a day. After a few years it became an integral part of a person. If the person then cleared his mind, by repeating the "Amidah," it produced a very high state of consciousness. This could also be true of other prayers. They became a meditative device like a mantra. Baal Shem Tov taught his followers to focus on simple acts of devotion carried out with deep concentration.

In Pearl Epstein's book on Kabbalah, she writes: "Like the Lurianic Kabbalists, the Hasid were very taken with the idea of man as God's necessary helpmate. Since the Absolute had constricted itself for man's sake, it was obligatory for man to purify the entire material world so that the light of the 'Ain Soph' could again radiate without the obstructions cast by illusion. The Hasid never doubted that his separation from God was illusory nor that his role in life consisted of stripping away the illusion. The ecstatic experience itself became his weapon for penetrating the barrier between his bodily and spiritual selves; expanded consciousness was his vehicle to God."[10]

Personal Thoughts of the Author

The "Collective Unconscious" of Jungian psychology conveys to us that human thinking is done under the influence of a great thought form. This Collective Unconscious is comparable to the Soul Consciousness, which in many ways is like a hologram. A hologram is a three dimensional picture, in which each small part is a replica of the whole. Therefore, if we carefully review the concept by C. G. Jung of the Collective Unconscious of the race, we are compelled to view individuals as being intrinsically linked with all life—that is, part of the great "group soul." As it has been said, "no man is an island unto himself."

Jung concluded that in this great Collective Unconscious was the deposit of the experiences of our ancestors. The conscious mind is held to be the outcropping of the unconscious. The springs of life are to be found in the underlying unconscious mind. The search of the mystic is to pass through this shell of existence and establish contact with the Inner Light, which is the element of Divinity, the hidden magnificence of all existence.

Though we try to invoke the Great Ones by chanting, prayers, and song, the music *they* can hear is the song of our lives. The Great Ones are drawn to us not only by the things we say, but by the things we do. The more we allow ourselves to become in tune with the infinite wisdom of our soul, the greater will be the understanding of the teachings.

We are at a spot in our evolution, a moment in time; we have had an awakening and are ready to turn ourselves over to our soul. Cabalah is the Rosetta Stone to help us understand the universe and the soul of man.

NOTES

1. Quotation of the Zohar taken from Dr. Philip S. Berg, *Kabbalah for the Layman* (Israel, Press of the Research Center of Kabbalah, 1981) page 120

2. Eliphas Levi, *Book of Splendours* (New York, Samuel Weiser, Inc. 1973) page 17

3. Aryeh Kaplan, *Meditation and Kabbalah* (York Beach, Maine, Samuel Weiser, Inc., 1982) page 41

4. Ben Zion Bokser, *The Jewish Mystical Tradition* (New York, The Pilgrim Press, 1981) page 16

5. Abraham ben Samuel Abulafia, 13th century Cabalist representing the "Prophetic Cabalah" (Spain, Italy)

6. Gershom Scholem, Kabbalah (Jerusalem, Kether Publishing House Ltd., 1974) page 410

7. Ibid. Aryeh Kaplan, *Meditation and Kabbalah,* page 201

8. Ibid. Aryeh Kaplan, *Meditation and Kabbalah,* page 218

9. Ibid. Gershom Scholem, *Kabbalah,* page 418

10. Pearl Epstein, *Kabbalah, the Way of the Jewish Mystic* (New York, Samuel Weiser, Inc., 1979) page 121

CONCLUSION

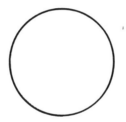

CONCLUSION

When we begin to study Cabalah, one of the first things we realize is that everything is interrelated. We become conscious of that connecting link between all of us. There is one thread that ties all of us together. Pillars of Light, Teachers of Immensity, and even Man himself are linked by this thread. While no two of us are exactly alike, there is still that link between us.

This connecting link that connects the High Teachers from the other side of the veil to all life on earth is called *The Creative Mind of the Soul*. It has been so named by a group of esoteric teachers bringing forth light and inspiration unto the earth plane. Therefore the connecting thread between you and God is the *soul*, which creates all.

You might say God is a consciousness, but God has a soul too. His connection to us is through our soul and his soul. The connection is there; we need only to be aware of it. We exist in our world, yet we must be part of another world in some facet of consciousness, and that connecting link is the Creative Mind of the Soul.

The soul is encapsulated or sealed, but it comes through to the conscious mind when we have a soul awakening. You ask, "How do we have a soul awakening?" The answer is through *experience.* The only difference between us and the Teachers on the other side of the veil is experience. They state we were all spewed forth from the AIN SOPH at the same time, yet some returned to the other side of the veil, and remain there permanently as Great Teachers of Light. But most of us on the earth plane keep returning back to Malkuth, over and over again.

Through their greater learning and experience, the Pillars of Light were able to create the world in which we live. Yet we are a thread of them, and they a thread of us. We grow stronger after every experience. Every man, woman, and child are what they are for the experience of being that. All are equal, yet we allow ourselves to be caught in the trap of thinking we are a who, a what, or a how.

We must learn to communicate with the spiritual plane. The physical is like the grave of the soul; and even if we live in the vibration of the physical, we must rise above it and be of the spiritual at the same time.

Do not be limited by the image of your physical body; be limitless like God. Take on the cloak of light. Allow your soul to come forth and guide your existence.

The veil of life at birth is placed between the mortal consciousness and the soul consciousness. But as the mortal learns, the veil diminishes. Open your heart and let the veil lift.

Your soul brought you into this consciousness so it can release you. But do not make the halls of the earth plane the highest for you. Rather seek to reach the higher halls of learning, while at the same time not being discontented with the present hall that your soul has chosen for you.

Once we understand all of these things, we may then cross through the last veil and become ourselves.

And now that you have stayed with us all the way to the end, let us see if the English language can tell us anything further about the connecting link—that which is called *"The Creative Mind of the Soul."* Its Tarot and Alpha numbers follow below:

	Tarot Number	Alpha Number
THE	28	33
CREATIVE	69	83
MIND	41	40
OF	21	21
THE	28	33
SOUL	48	67
Total Sum:	235	277
	We	B Christ (77)

What more can we ask!

APPENDIX

IMPORTANT CHARTS

GLOSSARY

BRIEF HISTORY OF CABALAH

BIBLIOGRAPHY

A TABLE OF HEBREW LETTERS AND NUMBERS

Number	Sound or Power.	Hebrew and Chaldee Letters.	Numerical Value.	Roman character by which expressed in this work.	Name.	Signification of Name.
			PLATE I.—TABLE OF HEBREW AND CHALDEE LETTERS.			
1.	a (soft breathing).	א	1. (Thousands are denoted by a larger letter; thus an Aleph larger than the rest of the letters among which it is, signifies not 1, but 1000.)	A.	Aleph.	Ox.
2.	b, bh (v).	ב	2.	B.	Beth.	House.
3.	g (hard), gh.	ג	3.	G.	Gimel.	Camel.
4.	d, dh (flat th).	ד	4.	D.	Daleth.	Door.
5.	h (rough breathing).	ה	5.	H.	He.	Window.
6.	v, u, o.	ו	6.	V.	Vau.	Peg, nail.
7.	z, dz.	ז	7.	Z.	Zayin.	Weapon, sword.
8.	ch (guttural).	ח	8.	CH.	Cheth.	Enclosure, fence.
9.	t (strong).	ט	9.	T.	Teth.	Serpent.
10.	i, y (as in yes).	י	10.	I.	Yod.	Hand.
11.	k, kh.	כ Final = ך	20. Final = 500	K.	Caph.	Palm of the hand.
12.	l.	ל	30.	L.	Lamed.	Ox-goad.
13.	m.	מ Final = ם	40. Final = 600	M.	Mem.	Water.
14.	n.	נ Final = ן	50. Final = 700	N.	Nun.	Fish.
15.	s.	ס	60.	S.	Samekh.	Prop, support.
16.	O, aa, ng (gutt.).	ע	70.	O.	Ayin.	Eye.
17.	p, ph.	פ Final = ף	80. Final = 800	P.	Pe.	Mouth.
18.	ts, tz, j.	צ Final = ץ	90. Final = 900	Tz.	Tzaddi.	Fishing-hook.
19.	q, qh (guttur.).	ק	100. (The finals are not always considered as bearing an increased numerical value.)	Q.	Qoph.	Back of the head.
20.	r.	ר	200.	R.	Resh.	Head.
21.	sh, s.	ש	300.	SH.	Shin.	Tooth.
22.	th, t.	ת	400.	TH.	Tau.	Sign of the cross.

The Hebrew Letters with Their English Equivalents According to MacGregor Mathers

THE ENGLISH LETTERS AND THEIR
NUMERICAL EQUIVALENTS

1	2	3	4	5	6	7	8	9
1 A	2 B	3 C	4 D	5 E	6 F	7 G	8 H	9 I
10 J	11 K	12 L	13 M	14 N	15 O	16 P	17 Q	18 R
19 S	20 T	21 U	22 V	23 W	24 X	25 Y	26 Z	

Letter	Alpha Number	Letter	Alpha Number	Letter	Alpha Number
A	1	J	10	S	19
B	2	K	11	T	20
C	3	L	12	U	21
D	4	M	13	V	22
E	5	N	14	W	23
F	6	O	15	X	24
G	7	P	16	Y	25
H	8	Q	17	Z	26
I	9	R	18		

TABLE OF CORRESPONDENCES OF HEBREW LETTERS
WITH TAROT CARDS

Hebrew Letter		Tarot No. on Card	Name of Tarot Card	Key Word
Aleph	(A)	1	The Magician	Magician
Beth	(B)	2	The High Priestess	Priestess
Gimel	(G)	3	The Empress	Empress
Daleth	(D)	4	The Emperor	Emperor
He	(H)	5	The Hierophant	Hierophant
Vav	(V)	6	The Lovers	Lovers
Zayin	(Z)	7	The Chariot	Chariot
Cheth	(Ch)	8	Strength	Strength
Teth	(T)	9	The Hermit	Hermit
Yod	(I)	10	The Wheel of Fortune	Wheel
Kaph	(K)	11	Justice	Justice
Lamed	(L)	12	The Hanged Man	Man
Mem	(M)	13	Death	Death
Nun	(N)	14	Temperance	Temperance
Samekh	(S)	15	The Devil	Devil
Ayin	(O)	16	The Tower	Tower
Pe	(P)	17	The Star	Star
Tzaddi	(Tz)	18	The Moon	Moon
Qoph	(Q)	19	The Sun	Sun
Resh	(R)	20	Judgement	Judgement
Shin	(Sh)	0	The Fool	Fool
Taw	(Th)	21	The World	World

22 Letters   22 Trumps

TABLE OF ONE-TO-ONE CORRESPONDENCE OF TAROT CARDS AND ENGLISH ALPHABET

English Letter	Alpha Number	Name of Tarot Card	Tarot Number	Key Word Alpha Number	Card Name Alpha Number
A	1	The *Emperor*	4	90	123
B	2	The *Wheel* of Fortune	10	53	206
C	3	The *Moon*	18	57	90
D	4	The *Devil*	15	52	85
E	5	The *Hierophant*	5	114	147
F	6	The High *Priestess*	2	130	195
G	7	*Justice*	11	87	87
H	8	The *Hermit*	9	73	106
I	9	The *Magician*	1	57	90
J	10	The *World*	21	72	105
K	11	The *King*	11	41	74
L	12	The *Knight*	12	69	102
M	13	*Death*	13	38	38
N	14	The Hanged *Man*	12	28	100
O	15	The *Sun*	19	54	87
P	16	The *Page*	16	29	62
Q	17	The *Queen*	17	62	95
R	18	The *Tower*	16	81	114
S	19	The *Star*	17	58	91
T	20	*Temperance*	14	100	100
U	21	The *Fool*	0	48	81
V	22	The *Lovers*	6	91	124
W	23	The *Chariot*	7	74	107
X	24	*Judgement*	20	99	99
Y	25	*Strength*	8	111	111
Z	26	The *Empress*	3	95	128

GLOSSARY

The following words and terms are provided for careful reflection in the study of Cabalah:

ABULAFIA, RABBI ABRAHAM BEN SAMUEL (1240–1290), Cabalist representing the "Prophetic Cabalah" (Spain, Italy)

ADAM KADMON, the first or Heavenly Man, the Manifested Logos, the Divine Androgyne. He represents the manifestation of our Body of Light which has the ability to create and teach all. This Light Body of Adam Kadmon is an extension of God. Each of us is said to mirror this archetypal figure.

ADONAI, a Hebrew word for God. Its meaning is similar to that of Jehovah, or IHVH.

AHIYE ASHER AHIYE, Hebrew words having the same meaning as "I AM THAT I AM." It is the knowing that the human-self and the God-Self are One.

AIN, Nothing, or Negative Existence. AIN equates to the Universal Essence.

AIN SOPH, the Limitless and Boundless, the Infinite State, the Spiritual Consciousness from which the emanations came forth. This is the primal state in which the soul of man is in perfect harmony with God. God, who is everywhere.

AIN SOPH AUR, Limitless Light, the aura that surrounds the physical body of the lesser entity of Man, and the greater entity of the Cosmos.

AKIBA, RABBI BEN JOSEPH, teacher of Rabbi Simeon ben Yohai, the author of the *Zohar*. He was the principal speaker in the "Lesser Heikhalot," one of the oldest cabalistic texts available.

ALPHA NUMBER, the numerical value of English words. Any word in the English language can be expressed as a number simply by spelling it, and substituting the values of the letters in their normal sequence: $A = 1$, $B = 2$, $C = 3$, etc.

AMIDAH, a Hebrew word for the silent portion of daily prayer.

APEX OF SERIES (as used in the mathematics of Phi), the first term at the top of the Pyramid/Tree of Life representing the letter A. The C term is always equal to the Apex term.

ARCANA, mysterious knowledge known to initiates, the basic divisions of the Tarot. The word is derived from the Latin root *arca*, meaning that which encloses or conceals.

BAAL SHEM TOV, ISRAEL (1700–1760), the founder of the Hasidic movement revival. Baal Shem Tov means "bearer of good name." His teachings were for everyone, not just the scholars.

BAHIR (Book of Brilliance), one of the oldest cabalistic books attributed to Rabbi Nehunia ben Hakana. It covers the theory of reincarnation, the feminine principle of God, and the Sephiroth.

BERASHITH, the first word in the Hebrew Bible, and the first word of Genesis. This is the Hebrew term for "In the beginning."

BINAH, 3rd Sephirah on the Tree of Life. It is located in the left-hand Pillar of Severity, sometimes referred to as the Pillar of Boaz. Binah means Understanding.

BOAZ, the shadowy Pillar of Darkness in the Masonic tradition. Its counterpart in the Hebrew Tree of Life is the Pillar of Severity. Symbolically, the Pillars of Boaz and Jachin stood on either side of the entrance to Solomon's Temple.

CHESED, 4th Sephirah on the Tree of Life, on the right-hand Pillar of Mercy. Chesed means Mercy or Love.

CHOKMAH, 2nd Sephirah on the Tree of Life. It heads the right-hand Pillar of Mercy, sometimes referred to as the Pillar of Jachin. Chokmah means Wisdom.

DAATH, the empty Sephirah in the Middle Pillar of the Tree of Life between Kether and Tiphareth. It sometimes represents the digit 0. Daath means Gnosis or Knowledge.

DEAD SEA SCROLLS (Scriptures), the sacred teachings of God used by the Qumran sect, a spiritual community that lived near the Dead Sea in Israel. The scrolls were discovered in a cave in 1947.

DECAGON, a geometric figure formed when ten triangles unite at their apexes, forming a ten-sided regular polygon. For Pythagoras, it was the symbol of the universe.

DEVEKUTH, the meditative state of cleaving to the divine.

ENOCH, the principal character in *The Book of Enoch*, a part of the Heikhalot literature which comes from the Book of Ezekiel. Enoch is a cobbler who dedicates his life to piety, and he is taken to heaven and turned into an angel called Metatron. This book is declared apocryphal, the term meaning secret book, one that belongs in the temple libraries.

FIBONACCI NUMBER, a term in a series of numbers named after Leonardo Fibonacci, a 12th century mathematician who found that nature counts differently than man.
Man counts 0, 1, 2, 3, 4, 5, 6, 7, 8, 9, 10. . . .
Nature counts 0, 1, 1, 2, 3, 5, 8, 13, 21, 34, 55. . . .

FOUR WORLDS, the four worlds of the Cabalah under the presidency of God (Yod He Vav He). They are arranged in four consecutive "Tree of Life" glyphs. These trees disclose the organization of the hierarchies controlling the destinies of all creation. The trees are the same in each of the four worlds, but the powers in the Sephirothic globes express themselves differently through the substances of each world. They are named as follows in the order of their manifestation: (1) Atziluth, (2) Briah, (3) Yetzirah, and (4) Assiah. The fourth world is the lowest world and represents the physical plane.

GEBURAH, 5th Sephirah on the left-hand Pillar of Severity. Its equivalent meaning in English is Severity, Strength, or Fortitude. It is located in the middle of the pillar, thus giving the pillar its name.

GEMATRIA, one of the three cabalistic disciplines used to decipher the hidden meaning of Scripture. Words of similar numerical values tend to be explanatory of each other is the basic law of Gematria.

GIKATALIA, RABBI JOSEPH (1270 A.D.), Spanish Cabalist who wrote *Gates of Light, Garden of Nut Trees,* and *Holy Letter.*

HAKANA, RABBI NEHUNIAH BEN, considered the author of the *Bahir.*

HASID, an adherent of Hasidism, a very pious person.

HASIDIC ASHKENAZI, German or Eastern European Hasidic Jews.

HASIDISM, a revivalist movement of Jewish mysticism in Germany and other parts of Europe in the Middle Ages. The name also refers to a cabalistic movement founded by Israel Baal Shem Tov in the first half of the 18th century.

HEIKHALOT, the "heavenly halls" seen during meditation by the early Jewish mystics. They refer to the temples as described by the prophet Ezekiel from his visions.

HOD, 8th Sephirah at the base of the left-hand Pillar of Severity. Hod means Glory or Splendor.

HOLOGRAM, a three-dimensional picture that is made on a photographic film or plate without the use of a camera. For viewing, the hologram is illuminated with coherent light from behind. Because of the uniqueness of the holographic process, the whole could be considered to be contained within each of its microscopic parts.

I AM THAT I AM, the name by which God desires to be known (Exodus 3:14). The covenant between the human-self and the God-Self. It is the knowing of one's true identity.

IHVH, the Tetragrammaton of the Hebrew letters *Yod He Vav He* (Yahweh), the English translation of which means LORD. Sometimes these Hebrew letters are transliterated into English as YHWH or JHVH.

JACHIN, the white Pillar of Light in the Masonic tradition. Its counterpart in the Hebrew Tree of Life is the right-hand Pillar of Mercy. Symbolically, the Pillars of Boaz and Jachin stood on either side of the entrance to Solomon's Temple.

KARMA, a universal law of cause and effect, which provides the soul with opportunities for mental, physical, and spiritual growth.

KAVVANAH, concentration accompanying prayer and the performance of ritual. It represents the one-pointedness necessary to receive awareness of the higher realms.

KETHER, 1st Sephirah at the top of the Middle Pillar of the Tree of Life. Kether means Crown. It represents the "I AM" of pure existence.

LEON, R. MOSES DE BEN SHEMTOV (1290 A.D.), famed Spanish Cabalist who contributed to and published the first complete volume of the *Zohar* (Book of Splendor). Modern-day scholars still do not agree as to how much of the actual writing of the *Zohar* was performed by him.

LURIA, ISAAC (1534–1572), founder of the Lurianic system of Cabalah in Safed, the cabalistic center in Galilee. He was known as the *Ari*, an acronym for the godly Rabbi Isaac, and his teachings have had a great influence in modern times. They were usually given orally, and were written down by Rabbi Hayyim Vital, his most celebrated student.

MACROCOSM, MICROCOSM, the greater universe of the Cosmos, and the lesser universe of Man. As above, so below. Man is considered to be created in the image of God. Therefore Man, the *microcosm*, is a reflection of God, the *macrocosm*.

MAIMONIDES, RABBI MOSES BEN MAIMON (1135–1204), born in Cordoba, Spain, and later to become the most important Jewish philosopher of the Middle Ages. His main philosophical work, *Guide to the Perplexed,* presents a rational Aristotelian view of Judaism.

MALKUTH, 10th Sephirah at the base of the Middle Pillar of the Tree of Life. Malkuth means Kingdom. It represents the physical world.

MANTRA, a set of sound patterns and thought forms used to harmonize one's outer consciousness with his inner consciousness of Light. Mantras are holy energy forms of meditation that can charge the body with the power of the Divine Mind.

MEDITATION, sometimes called prayer or contemplation. The approach to Deity in word and thought. It is an attempt to activate the Divine Consciousness in the body so that its positive energy can be used for the benefit of oneself or others. When we concentrate upon a thought or idea, it tends to become action and self-realization. Therefore, the invocation of light can provide balance and harmony between the inner and outer worlds.

MERKABAH, the Chariot associated with Ezekiel's vision of the Divine Throne (Book of Ezekiel). The Merkabah teachings are some of the earliest ones in the Cabalah. The Chariot is the vehicle of divine light used to reach the Divine Mind.

MIDDLE PILLAR, the middle pillar on the Tree of Life, balancing the negative and positive energies that otherwise would exist between the Pillar of Severity (Boaz) on the left, and the Pillar of Mercy (Jachin) on the right. The middle pillar is called the Pillar of Mildness.

NETZACH, 7th Sephirah at the base of the right-hand Pillar of Mercy. Its equivalent meaning in English is Victory, but in another sense it means Firmness.

NOTARIQON, one of the three cabalistic disciplines used to decipher the hidden meaning of Scripture. In Notariqon (abbreviations), the initial letters of the words in a phrase can be used to form another word that signifies the whole.

PENTACLE, a five-pointed star used as a magical symbol. Usually it is inscribed in a circle. It has the same meaning as a pentagram.

PENTAGON, a five-sided regular polygon.

PENTAGRAM, the familiar five-pointed star in the shape of a pentacle. When a pentagram is divided internally into many triangular parts, it becomes a treasure-trove of Phi ratios. The arms of a pentagram cut each other in Phi proportions (the Golden Mean), and the process can be continued indefinitely.

PHI (also known as the Divine Proportion, the Golden Mean, Golden Section, or Golden Cut). The division of a line into two unequal parts, so that the lesser is to the greater as the greater is to the whole.

PHI MEAN, the midpoint in a Phi series of numbers (see Fibonacci numbers), that separates the positive terms (physical consciousness) from those that are alternately positive and negative (spiritual consciousness).

PILLAR OF LIGHT, the consciousness of Man in the highest realm of the Spiritual Consciousness. Light means wisdom, so you could call one who is in that state a Pillar of Wisdom. The Alpha number of "Pillar" is 68, the same as "Logos" (68). Therefore, through the laws of Gematria, the use of the word "Pillar" further enhances the meaning of the word "Logos" (the controlling principle in the Universe).

PYRAMID/TREE OF LIFE, the primary glyph of the English Cabalah. A cross section through the center of the Great Pyramid at Giza (a Phi pyramid) is divided into an infinite number of Phi triangles.

PYTHAGORAS, Greek philosopher (569–500 b.c.) who observed certain numerical patterns in the harmonies of nature. He later made a science out of these observations, and contributed much towards our present understanding of number, music, and harmony. He is probably best known by the mathematical theorem that bears his name, and his "music of the spheres."

QLIPHOTH, the evil and adverse Sephiroth (their reverse sides) that represent unbalanced and destructive forces. They are sometimes called shells, and they are brought into manifestation by Man himself, through his mortal mind and negative thinking.

Thus created, they then enclose him in their negative light, and limit his spiritual development.

SEPHER YETZIRAH (Book of Formation), one of the oldest cabalistic writings. The work has been attributed to Abraham the Patriarch. It describes the creation of the world through the powers inherent in the ten Sephiroth and the 22 letters of the Hebrew alphabet.

SEPHIRAH, SEPHIROTH, the singular and plural forms of the Hebrew word for the spheres or vessels through which the light of God is emanated down to Man. The Sephiroth are linked to each other on the Tree of Life by paths (canals or roads) along which the divine emanations travel.

SEPHIROTHIC TREE OF LIFE, the primary glyph of the Hebrew Cabalah. The ten Sephiroth are shown connected by 22 paths, the combination of which brings forth the 32 wonderful paths of wisdom described in the *Sepher Yetzirah*. Each path represents a different experience that man must undergo in his journey towards enlightenment.

SHEKHINAH, the feminine aspect of God, the Divine Presence among men. The idea of the dual nature of God (the masculine and feminine principle) appears in the *Bahir*, the first Hebrew work to take this into account.

TALMUD, a compilation of the various discussions of the Palestinian sages over a period of centuries. The *Talmud* is the written form of Hebrew law. It is the main work of Hebrew scholars.

TAROT, the Book of Tarot, a deck of cards containing 78 universal symbols. These symbols express all the laws of Man, God, and the Universe.

TEMURA, one of the three cabalistic disciplines used to decipher the hidden meaning of Scripture. In Temura (permutations or anagrams), the letters in any word may be rearranged to make another word, which also tends to explain its meaning. But the rearrangements of the letters will have no effect upon the numerical value of the original word. The other two cabalistic disciplines are Gematria and Notariqon.

TEN COMMANDMENTS, the two tablets of the Law which Moses brought down from Mount Sinai. They were inscribed in two groups of five, in columnar form. They can be compared to the ten Sephiroth.

TETRACTYS, the Pythagorean symbol of ten dots, or commas, arranged in four rows within an equilateral triangle. These, too, could be compared to the ten Sephiroth. The basic idea that they portrayed was that the sum of the first *four* integers equates to ten $(1 + 2 + 3 + 4 = 10)$.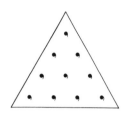

TETRAGRAMMATON, the four Hebrew letters *Yod He Vav He* which comprise the Divine Name (Yahweh). See IHVH.

TIPHARETH, 6th Sephirah at the exact center of the Tree of Life, balanced between its upper and lower parts in the middle Pillar of Mildness. Tiphareth means Beauty.

TORAH, the Pentateuch, the first part of Jewish Scripture contained in the five books of Moses. Torah means Law. These are its limited definitions. However in recent years it has come to mean the total doctrine of Judaism, written and oral.

TZIMTZUM, the self constriction of God's Light. Basically, it is the concept that God "withdrew" His Light, forming a vacant space in which creation could take place.

UNWRITTEN CABALAH, that part of the Cabalah which was never put into writing, but only communicated orally from Teacher to disciple. But, eventually, that which was "unwritten" becomes "written" as new information is gradually published from time to time, and when the powers that be are ready to have it revealed.

VEILS, metaphysical walls which we create by our negative actions. The veils don't let the light of God come in, and therefore limit the spiritual growth of the individual.

YESOD, 9th Sephirah located on the middle pillar, just above Malkuth. The English translation of Yesod is *Foundation*.

YOHAI, RABBI SIMEON BEN (2nd century, A.D.), the reputed true author of the *Zohar*. After being sentenced to death by the Romans, Rabbi Simeon spent twelve years hiding in a cave in Palestine, where he was able to receive the heavenly doctrine and communicate it to his disciples. He became known as the "Sacred Light."

ZAKKAI, RABBI JOCHANAN BEN (50 A.D.), the father of Merkabah mysticism which evolved from Ezekiel's visions in the Book of Ezekiel. He was the youngest disciple of Rabbi Hillel who prophesied the destruction of the Temple.

ZOHAR (Book of Splendor), one of the main works of cabalistic literature. Although basically a commentary on the five books of Moses, it also contains valuable other information on the Sephiroth, the doctrine of creation, and the Merkabah mysticism of numbers and letters. Its authorship is attributed to Rabbi Simeon ben Yohai.

BRIEF HISTORY OF CABALAH

Jewish mysticism covers the last two thousand years.
It can be divided into the following periods:

1. **Period of Merkabah Mysticism** (1st millennium): The development of Cabalah had its beginnings in the esoteric teachings of
   the Jews of Palestine and Egypt, in the era which saw the birth
   of Christianity, the first millennium. Yet the teachings can be
   traced back to earlier times of oral knowledge, and on the monu-
   ments and in the sacred scrolls and hieroglyphics of all nations.
   It is generally accepted by Cabalists that the various doctrines
   found in the *Sepher Yetzirah*, the *Zohar*, and the *Bahir*, were put
   into writing during this period by certain students after discussion
   with a teacher, probably the Rabbi Simeon ben Yochai. Then the
   many manuscripts were copied and circulated throughout Europe,
   while being carefully guarded by esotericists.

2. **Period of Hasidism in Germany** (1150–1300): This movement
   reached its peak in the second half of the 12th and first part of
   the 13th century, but it continued to have repercussions well into
   the 16th century, particularly in the Judaism of the Ashkenazi
   world. That movement was known as the Hasidei Askenaz. In
   Provence, southern France, there was a contemporaneous growth
   of Hasidism with Germany. It was in Provence that the *Bahir*
   reappeared (1150–1200).

3. **Period of Cabalah in Spain** (1200–1492): The Jews were expelled from Spain in 1492 by Queen Isabella and King Ferdinand. While the Cabalistic center was in Spain, the greatly inspired work of Rabbi Moses de Leon of Guadalajara was published. He collected together the different manuscripts of the disciples of Rabbi Simeon ben Yohai, and edited and arranged them in book form as a complete work, *The Zohar*. But the *Zohar* was for the initiates only, the elite of the Jewish scholars; it was the esoteric doctrine. After the expulsion of the Jews from Spain in 1492, the refugees settled in North Africa, Italy, and the eastern Mediterranean. This caused Cabalah to spread to wider circles and become more dominant as an expression of deity.

4. **Period of Cabalah in Safed, Palestine** (1500–1650): A major cabalistic renaissance took place in the 16th century in Safed, the upper part of Galilee. A group of scholars and mystics, mainly of Spanish origin, settled here. The most influential of them was Isaac Luria, whose teachings became the dominant form of esoteric wisdom.

5. **Period of the Shabbathean Movement** (1665–1800): The doctrines of this period soon developed into a mystical heresy and rendered the Cabalah suspect. The Lurianic Cabalah provided the theological background for this 17th century messianic movement, which was connected with Sabbatai Zevi and his prophet, Nathan of Gaza. This was the only messianic movement to engulf the whole of Jewry—from England to Persia, from Germany to Morocco, from Poland to the Yemen. Sabbatai Zevi was called "messiah."

6. **Period of Hasidism in Eastern Europe** (since 1750): The 18th century mystical revival was initiated by Israel Baal Shem Tov, who reestablished the Hasidic movement and it still remains active today. The foundation of Baal Shem Tov's wisdom is based on Lurianic teachings. Baal Shem Tov taught that joy and happiness are the way to achieve union with God.

7. **Period of the Development of Christian Cabalism** (17th and 18th centuries): Jewish mysticism was relatively unknown to Christian scholars until Knorr von Rosenroth published *Kabbala Denudata* in 1677. This work was a translation, in Latin, of certain parts

of the *Zohar*, and it remained as the principal source for all non-Jewish literature on Cabalah until the end of the 18th century. Yet the early Christian Cabalists, often instructed by Jewish scholars, possessed a sound knowledge of the subject. We have only to look at the works of Pico della Mirandola and Reuchlin to know that this is so. 17th century England produced Thomas Vaughan, Robert Fludd, and Henry More.

8. **Modern Period** (19th and 20th centuries): Modern-day non-Jewish Cabalism began in France with the works of M. Court de Gébelin, Eliphas Levi, Adolphe Franck, and others. The first book to be published in English relative to the doctrines of Cabalah was in the form of an essay by Christian D. Ginsburg. This was in 1863 when he brought the subject before the Literary and Philosophical Society of Liverpool. That was all that was needed. In practically no time at all many other books appeared, by numerous authors, and the basic principles of Cabalah began to be taught in many esoteric societies throughout Europe and America.

BIBLIOGRAPHY

The bibliography that follows contains just a few of the many books that are available on the subject, and in no way is it intended to be an exhaustive list. All it represents is a simple compilation of books which the author has found informative and highly recommends.

BERG, DR. PHILLIP S. *Kabbalah for the Layman* (Israel, Press of the Research Center of Kabbalah, 1982)

BLAVATSKY, H. P. *Secret Doctrine* Volume IV (Adyar, India, Theosophical Publishing House, 1962 ed.)

BOKSER, BEN ZION. *The Jewish Mystical Tradition* (New York, The Pilgrim Press, 1981)

BUTLER, W. E. *Magic and the Qabalah* (New York, The Aquarian Press, Samuel Weiser, Inc. 1972)

CROWLEY, ALEISTER. *777 and other Qabalistic writings of Aleister Crowley including Gematria and Sepher Sephiroth.* Edited and Introduction by Israel Regardie (New York, Samuel Weiser, 1973)

EISEN, WILLIAM. *The English Cabalah*, Volume I, The Mysteries of Pi (Marina Del Rey, Calif., DeVorss & Co., 1980)

EISEN, WILLIAM. *The English Cabalah*, Volume II, The Mysteries of Phi (Marina Del Rey, Calif., DeVorss & Co., 1982)

EISEN, WILLIAM. *The Essence of the Cabalah* (Marina Del Rey, Calif., DeVorss & Co., 1984)

EPSTEIN, PEARL. *Kabbalah the Way of the Jewish Mystic* (New York, hardcover, Doubleday & Co., Inc., 1978; paperback, N.Y. Samuel Weiser Inc., 1979)

FORTUNE, DION. *The Mystical Qabalah* (New York, Alta Gaia Books, 1935)

GINSBURG, CHRISTIAN D. *The Essenes, Their History and Doctrines and The Kabbalah; Its Doctrines, Development, and Literature* (New York, MacMillian Co. 1865, 1956)

FRANCK, ADOLPHE. *The Kabbalah* (New York, Bell Publishing Co., 1940)

GRAY, EDEN. *A Complete Guide to the Tarot* (New York, Crown Publishers, 1970)

GRAY, WILLIAM G. *The Ladder of Lights* (U.S.A., Samuel Weiser, Inc., 1968)

GRAY, WILLIAM G. *The Talking Tree* (York Beach, Maine, Samuel Weiser, Inc., 1977)

HALEVI, ZEV BEN SHIMON. *An Introduction to Cabala, Tree of Life* (New York, Samuel Weiser, Inc., 1972)

HALEVI, ZEV BEN SHIMON. *Kabbalah, Tradition of Hidden Knowledge* (England, Thames and Hudson, 1979)

HALL, MANLY PALMER. *Collected Writings, Volume 3, Essays and Poems* (Los Angeles, The Philosophical Research Society, Inc., 1962)

HALL, MANLY PALMER. *The Secret Teachings of All Ages* (Los Angeles, The Philosophical Research Society, Inc., 1928 and 1978)

HOELLER, STEPHAN A. *The Gnostic Jung and Seven Sermons to the Dead* (Wheaton, Ill. U.S.A./Madras, India/London, England, 1982)

HOELLER, STEPHAN A. *The Royal Road*, A Manual of Kabalistic Meditations on the Tarot (Wheaton, Illinois U.S.A., Theosophical Publishing House, 1975)

HOFFMAN, EDWARD. *The Way of Splendor, Jewish Mysticism and Modern Psychology* (Boulder & London, Shambhala, 1981)

JUNG, CARL GUSTAV. *Man and His Symbols* (New York, Doubleday & Co., Inc., 1964, 1970)

JUNG, CARL GUSTAV. *The Collected Works of C. G. Jung*, Vol. 12, Editors: Herbert Read, Michael Fordham, M.D.M.R.C.P., Gerhard Adler, Ph.D., William Mcguire, executive editor, Translated by R.F.C. Hull (New Jersey, Bollingen Foundation, Princeton University Press, Second edition 1968, First Princeton/Bollingen printing, 1980)

KAPLAN, ARYEH. *The Bahir*, Attributed to Rabbi Nehunia ben HaKana, master of the first century esoteric school. Translation, Introduction and Commentary by Aryeh Kaplan (New York, Samuel Weiser, Inc. 1979)

KAPLAN, ARYEH. *Meditation and Kabbalah* (York Beach, Maine, Samuel Weiser, Inc. 1982)

LEVI, ELIPHAS. *Transcendental Magic* (London, William Rider & Son, 1923) (New York, Samuel Weiser, Inc. 1974)

LEVI, ELIPHAS. *Book of Splendours* (New York, Samuel Weiser, Inc. 1973)

MATHERS, MAC GREGOR. *The Kabbalah Unveiled* (New York, Samuel Weiser, Inc. 1968)

ODEGURG, HUGO. ed. and tran. *3 Enoch or the Hebrew Book of Enoch* (England, University Press, 1928)

PAPUS (Dr. Gerard Encausse), *The Qabalah Secret Tradition of the West* (England, Thorsons Publishers Limited, 1977; New York, Samuel Weiser, Inc.)

PONCE, CHARLES. *Kabbalah, An Introduction and Illumination for the World Today* (Wheaton, Ill./Madras, India/London, England, 1973)

REGARDIE, ISRAEL. *A Garden of Pomegranates* (St. Paul, Minn. Llewellyn Publications, 1932, 1970, 1971, 1974, 1978)

SAFRAN, ALEXANDRE. *The Kabbalah, Law and Mysticism in the Jewish Tradition* (New York, Jerusalem, Feldheim Publishers, 1975)

SCHOLEM, GERSHOM G. *Jewish Gnosticism, Merkabah Mysticism and Talmudic Tradition* (U.S.A., The Jewish Theological Seminary of America, 1960)

SCHOLEM, GERSHOM G. *Kabbalah* (Jersusalem, Keter Publishing House, Ltd., 1974)

SCHOLEM, GERSHOM G. *Zohar—The Book of Splendor, Basic Readings from the Kabbalah* (New York, Schocken Books, 1949)

SUARES, CARLO. *The Cipher of Genesis, The Original Code of the Qabala as applied to Scriptures* (Boulder & London, Shambhala Publications, 1967, 1970)

WAITE, ARTHUR EDWARD. *The Holy Kabbalah* (New Jersey, University Books, 1975)

WAITE, ARTHUR EDWARD. *Pictorial Key to the Tarot* (New York, University Books, reprinted 1959, originally published 1910)

WESTCOTT, WILLIAM WYNN. *The Kabalah* (England, Percy Lund Humphries Co. Ltd., 1910, 1926)

WESTCOTT, WILLIAM WYNN. *Sepher Yetzirah The Book of Formation and the Thirty Two Paths of Wisdom* (New York, Samuel Weiser, Inc. First Pub. 1887, Reprinted 1975)